ART AND SOCIAL JUSTICE EDUCATION

"This book will be enthusiastically embraced by all who understand that art education can be a powerful way to create citizens who are engaged participants in society. It moves us far beyond art education as holiday decorations for the classroom and explores the power of the arts to raise critical issues of social justice."

Mara Sapon-Shevin, Syracuse University

"If I can't dance, I don't want to be part of your classroom. A classroom without drawing is not a classroom worth having. If there won't be singing in the classroom, I won't be coming. How can my imagination grow beyond the ugliness of today, if you don't allow me to paint? *Art and Social Justice Education* makes the case, not only intellectually, but emotionally. These are the two ways forward: head and heart, hand in hand."

Vijay Prashad, Trinity College

"This anthology evokes ingenious images of teaching and learning. It presents in a compelling and well-argued fashion the undeniable affinity between educators striving to achieve a more equitable society and artists seeking to better inhabit the world. A must-read for all those engaged in the evolving work for change."

Flávia Bastos, School of Art, University of Cincinnati

Therese Quinn is Chair and Associate Professor of Art Education at the School of the Art Institute of Chicago.

John Ploof is Professor of Art Education at the School of the Art Institute of Chicago.

Lisa Hochtritt is Chair of Art Education at Rocky Mountain College of Art + Design in Denver, Colorado.

ART AND SOCIAL JUSTICE EDUCATION

Culture as Commons

Edited by
Therese Quinn, John Ploof,
and Lisa Hochtritt

NEW YORK AND LONDON

Please visit the Companion Website at www.routledge.com/cw/quinn

First published 2012
by Routledge
711 Third Avenue, New York, NY 10017

Simultaneously published in the UK
by Routledge
2 Park Square, Milton Park, Abingdon, Oxon OX14 4RN

Routledge is an imprint of the Taylor & Francis Group, an informa business

© 2012 Taylor & Francis

The right of the editors to be identified as the authors of the editorial material, and of the authors for their individual chapters, has been asserted in accordance with sections 77 and 78 of the Copyright, Designs and Patents Act 1988.

All rights reserved. No part of this book may be reprinted or reproduced or utilized in any form or by any electronic, mechanical, or other means, now known or hereafter invented, including photocopying and recording, or in any information storage or retrieval system, without permission in writing from the publishers.

Trademark notice: Product or corporate names may be trademarks or registered trademarks, and are used only for identification and explanation without intent to infringe.

Library of Congress Cataloging in Publication Data
Art and social justice education: culture as commons/edited by Therese Quinn, John Ploof, and Lisa Hochtritt.
  p. cm.
  Includes bibliographical references and index.
  1. Education—Social aspects—United States. 2. Art in education—Social aspects. 3. Arts—Study and teaching. 4. Social justice—Study and teaching. 5. Teaching—Social aspects—United States. I. Quinn, Therese. II. Ploof, John. III. Hochtritt, Lisa.
LC191.4.A763 2011
372.5'044—dc23   2011027006

ISBN: 978-0-415-87906-4 (hbk)
ISBN: 978-0-415-87907-1 (pbk)
ISBN: 978-0-203-85247-7 (ebk)

Typeset in Bembo and Stone Sans
by Florence Production Ltd, Stoodleigh, Devon

Printed and bound in the United States of America on acid-free paper by Walsworth Publishing Company, Marceline, MO

CONTENTS

Foreword: The Introduction   xi
Bill Ayers and Maxine Greene, as told by
Ryan Alexander-Tanner

Acknowledgments   xvii

Editors' Introduction   xviii
Therese Quinn, John Ploof, and Lisa Hochtritt

Part I—The Commons: Redistribution of Resources and Power   1

   Introduction to Part I: Yours as Much as Mine   3
   Therese Quinn

 1 Justseeds: An Artists' Cooperative   6
   David Darts

 2 Heidi Cody: Letters to the World and the ABCs of
   Visual Culture   9
   Kevin Tavin

 3 Kutiman: It's the Mother of All Funk Chords   11
   K. Wayne Yang

4 ToroLab: Border Research Gone Molecular   14
   Nato Thompson

5 Mequitta Ahuja: Afrogalaxy   17
   Romi Crawford

6 Emily Jacir: The Intersection of Art and Politics 19
   Edie Pistolesi

7 Paula Nicho Cúmez: Crossing Borders   22
   Kryssi Staikidis

8 Rafael Trelles: Cleaning Up the Stain of Militarism 25
   Nicolas Lampert

9 Experience, Discover, Interpret, and Communicate: Material Culture Studies and Social Justice in Art Education   28
   Doug Blandy

10 Educational Crisis: An Artistic Intervention   35
   Dipti Desai and Elizabeth Koch

11 Social Media/Social Justice: The (Creative) Commons and K-12 Art Education   41
   Robert W. Sweeny and Hannah Johnston

Part II—Our Cultures: Recognition and Representation   47

   Introduction to Part II: Build Something Fresh   49
   John Ploof

12 Kaisa Leka: Confusing the Disability/Ability Divide   53
   Carrie Sandahl

13 Darrel Morris: Men Don't Sew in Public   56
   Dónal O'Donoghue

14 Nicholas Galanin: Imaginary Indian and the Indigenous Gaze   59
   Anne-Marie Tupuola

15	Kimsooja: The Performance of Universality *Dalida María Benfield*	62
16	Xu Bing: Words of Art *Buzz Spector*	65
17	Bernard Williams: Art as Reinterpretation, Identity as Art *James Haywood Rolling, Jr.*	68
18	Hock E Aye Vi Edgar Heap of Birds: Beyond the Chief *Elizabeth Delacruz*	71
19	Samuel Fosso: Queering Performances of Realness *G. E. Washington*	74
20	Cultural Conversations in Spiral Curriculum *Olivia Gude*	76
21	Arts Making as an Act of Theory *Miia Collanus and Tiina Heinonen*	83
22	Pedagogy, Collaboration, and Transformation: A Conversation with Brett Cook *Korina Jocson and Brett Cook*	89

Part III—Toward Futures: Social and Personal Transformation — 95

	Introduction to Part III: The Next Big Thing *Lisa Hochtritt*	97
23	Harrell Fletcher: Shaping a New Social *Juan Carlos Castro*	101
24	Pinky & Bunny: Critical Pedagogy 2.0 *Steven Ciampaglia*	104
25	La Pocha Nostra: Practicing Mere Life *Jorge Lucero*	107
26	Future Farmers: Leaping Over the Impossible Present *A. Laurie Palmer*	110

27 Appalshop: Learning from Rural Youth Media   113
    Maritza Bautista

28 Navjot Altaf: What Public, Whose Art?   116
    Manisha Sharma

29 The Chiapas Photography Project: You Can't Unsee It   119
    Lisa Yun Lee

30 Dilomprizulike: Art as Political Agency   122
    Raimundo Martins

31 In Search of Clean Water and Critical Environmental Justice:
    Collaborative Artistic Responses Through the Possibilities
    of Sustainability and Appropriate Technologies   124
    B. Stephen Carpenter, II and Marissa Muñoz

32 Opening Spaces for Subjectivity in an Urban Middle-School
    Art Classroom: A Dialogue between Theory and Practice   131
    Carol Culp and Rubén Gaztambide-Fernández

33 Story Drawings: Revisiting Personal Struggles, Empathizing
    with "Others"   136
    Sharif Bey

Part IV—Voices of Teachers   **143**

Introduction to Part IV: Art Matters   145
Graeme Sullivan

34 Holding the Camera   150
    Maura Nugent

35 The Streets Are Our Canvas: Skateboarding, Hip-Hop,
    and School   153
    Keith "K-Dub" Williams

36 The Zine Teacher's Dilemma   156
    Jesse Senechal

37 Miracle on 79th Street: Using Community as Curriculum   160
    Delaney Gersten Susie

38	Public School, Public Failure, Public Art? *Bert Stabler*	164
39	Animating the Bill of Rights *William Estrada*	168
40	Think Twice, Make Once *Anne Thulson*	172
41	Art History and Social Justice in the Middle-School Classroom *Kimberly Lane*	176
42	Whatever Comes Next Will Be Made and Named by Us *Vanessa López-Sparaco*	180

About the Contributors	185
Figure Credits and Permissions	193
Index	198

Foreword xiii

xiv Foreword

Foreword xv

ACKNOWLEDGMENTS

In the spirit of the commons, we acknowledge this book as the product of collective creative labor. We wish to thank our family, friends, teachers, artists, cultural workers and students who inspire us to work for art and social justice, and our many colleagues who generously offered us their time for feedback and suggestions. Finally, we offer many thanks to Naomi Silverman and all at Routledge who supported this project.

This publication was created with the support of the School of the Art Institute of Chicago and the Rocky Mountain College of Art + Design.

EDITORS' INTRODUCTION

It's a Movement, So Start Moving: Art Education for Social Justice

Therese Quinn, John Ploof, and Lisa Hochtritt

The poet Gwendolyn Brooks (1968/2005) reminds us that art is "not an old shoe," soft and comfortable. Often, she claims, "Art hurts. Art urges voyages—and it is easier to stay at home." But the alternative is devastating, a loss for individuals and for societies. In her poem *Boy Breaking Glass*, Brooks (1987) describes a child "Whose broken window is a cry of art" and imagines his cry:

> I shall create! If not a note, a hole.
> If not an overture, a desecration.

Today, in many schools, the arts are being stripped from the curriculum through testing imperatives leading to, as Brooks warns, disastrous consequences for our communities. But, at the same time, in classrooms everywhere arts educators are fighting for the rights of young people to be both creative and engaged citizens.

Beto Sepúlveda, one such teacher, created a project about political poster art for an elementary school. His students, primarily Latino, studied the history of this art form and then the class chose a topic for their prints—immigration. Next, Beto taught the group how to enlarge the images, and they created banners and large posters to carry at Chicago's first immigrants' rights march. Either of the first two steps might have been logical places to end the project, but Beto extended it in a way that is emblematic of teaching focused on justice. Aware that some parents and school staff would not be able to attend the march because of their undocumented status and work conflicts, the students and teacher decided to bring the day's events back to school. At the major march and rally they videotaped interviews with participants, and the resulting movie was shown at a school assembly to which the entire school community was invited. This project is an

Pedagogical Factory: Exploring Strategies for an Educated City, 2007, installation view at Hyde Park Art Center, Chicago. The Stockyard Institute, founded by Jim Duignan critically explored intersections between art, education, and the city. Working with other artists, collaboratives, and groups, such as The Center for Urban Pedagogy (New York), rum46 (Denmark), Think Tank (Philadelphia), Artlink (UK), and AREA Chicago: Art, Research, Education & Activism (Chicago), the project explored overlaps between education, economics, art, and activism.

example of the way that teachers can combine lessons from contemporary art and activism, and good pedagogy—that art and action can happen anywhere and context is everything.

This book is a collective effort and fully co-authored; the three of us came to its topics through years of working with students in the arts and education, and through our understandings that social change is possible through shared practice and ideas. Even with over 80 contributors, there are many more artists, educators, culture workers, and students that we wish could have been included.

Iris Marion Young's (1990) and Nancy Fraser's (1997) thinking influenced the organizational structure of this book. We devised four sections interpreted through lenses of social justice and contemporary art education: The Commons: Redistribution of Resources and Power; Our Cultures: Recognition and Representation; Toward Futures: Social and Personal Transformation; and Voices of Teachers. Each section includes art and writing intended to forward ideas of contemporary art and social justice.

The collection contributes to the evolution of the field of art education by moving beyond the dominant discipline-based art education (DBAE), and expressive and visual culture paradigms, by offering examples of art education that are engaged with context (the teacher and students' surroundings), contemporary art (current forms and perspectives) and critical social issues (the "going" world and abiding justice-related concerns). In particular, we highlight how creativity, when supported through education, can incite social change. Our critical framing essays propose, however, that change is not neutral; like education, it can be for something and against something else. Our book's premise is that art can contribute in a wide range of ways to the work of envisioning and creating a more just world.

There are many different ways of conceptualizing "social justice" within education. For example, Quinn (2006) writes that social justice art education is utopian *and* practical; it looks ahead to the more democratic society we can dream up and create in our classrooms, and at the same time it is grounded in the lives and concerns of our students. Ayers and Quinn (2005) also note that teaching for social justice is "always more possibility than accomplishment" (p. viii) but propose that it includes these themes: democracy, activism, history, public space, self-awareness, social literacy, and imagination.

From social theory more broadly, we take ideas about the goals of social justice put forth by Young (1990) and Fraser (1997), in which they delineate two primary aspects of justice. For Young, these are the "distributive," which is a traditional, necessary, and (she claims) inadequate way of conceiving of social justice that looks solely at the equitable allocation of material goods, and the "cultural," which acknowledges that social conditions are shaped not only by class and labor, but by other social structures including sexual identity, race, gender, and other aspects of culture (pp. 14–16). Similarly, Fraser has argued that the goals of social justice are "redistribution and recognition" (pp. 13–16). Both acknowledge the need for social justice movements to attend to economic and cultural realms. In other words, working for social justice through education and other ways requires attention to the complex contexts of people's lives, and then engaged responses aimed at change.

Because no book can address all ideas, and following the lead of Young and Fraser, we narrowed our focus to three major themes: The Commons—shared access to creative practice and art; Our Cultures—nurturing the ways we have developed to live in community; and Toward Futures—imagining and acting to change our world. In these sections we propose an arts education for social justice that moves away from doing things *for* people and toward doing things in solidarity *with* them. If we accept Hyde's (2010) definition of a commons as "a kind of property in which more than one person has a right of action" (p. 43), how can we understand our role in managing this common resource? To this point, we urge an arts education that aims at individual and collective transformation.

Frederick Douglass said, "knowledge unfits a child to be a slave" (1987, p. 92). In our paraphrase of his insight, art education prepares its participants for freedom; it invites, as poet Jayne Cortez (1996) expressed it, visions of "somewhere in advance of nowhere." In fact, many artists and scholars writing about art and education have expressed similar ideas.

For example, Dewey (1934), Greene (1995), and others have influenced strands within art education that address the importance of linking the arts to social change. These perspectives have been articulated as social reconstructionist (Freedman, 1994; Hicks, 1994; Stuhr, 1994), multicultural (Cahan & Kocur, 1996; Desai, 2003; New Museum, 2010), and critical art education, described as "explicitly in the service of social transformation" (Siegesmund, quoted in Holloway & Krensky, 2001, p. 361). In addition, social justice movements including feminism (Collins & Sandell, 1996), lesbian and gay liberation (Lampela & Check, 2003), and disability rights (Blandy, 1994, 1999) are reflected in art education literature. However, despite the availability of these examples, art education in most of the United States' schools is still dominated by "formalist/modernist model[s], in particular, Discipline-based Art Education, in which aesthetics is taught disconnected from its social context" (Holloway & Krensky, 2001, p. 359; see also Alexander & Day, 1991). Other art educators, like Gaudelius and Speirs (2002), argue for an "issues-based approach to the teaching of art" (p. 1) that includes contemporary art and topics. Finally, Dewhurst (2010) has proposed an inclusive and process-oriented definition of justice-focused arts education:

> While people often assume that social justice art education must be based on controversial or overtly political issues (i.e. race, violence, discrimination, etc.), this is not always the case. Rather, as long as the process of making art offers participants a way to construct knowledge, critically analyze an idea, and take action in the world, then they are engaged in the practice of social justice artmaking.
>
> (p. 7)

The practice of contemporary artists can inform particular ways of knowing that are germane to social justice art education. For example, relational art provides "a set of artistic practices which take as their theoretical and practical point of departure the whole of human relations and their social context, rather than independent and private space" (Bourriaud, 2002, p. 113). Contemporary art practices, such as those at the Pedagogical Factory, an exhibition at the Hyde Park Arts Center, explore current movements between critical practices of social art and pedagogy, and pose questions about relationships between urban life and learning. Rogoff (2010) describes related slippages that extend between the work of an increasing number of artists, educators, and curators. These include:

> "knowledge production", "research", "education", "open ended production" and "self organized pedagogies"—all of which seem to have converged into a set of parameters for some renewed facet of production. Although quite different in their genesis, methodology and protocols, it seems that some perceived proximity to "knowledge economies" has rendered all of these terms part and parcel of a certain liberalizing shift within the world of contemporary arts practices.
>
> *(p. 34)*

With this book we offer a vision of art education fully vested in contemporary arts practices and the hope and possibilities of social justice themes. As Disu (2008) (aka FM Supreme) reminds us, we all have a role to play in building the commons:

> Fighting for the youth,
> like Jane Addams on my shoulder,
> the movement starts with you,
> so start walking till it's over.
> This is a movement,
> so start moving.

These lyrics and the contributors in this anthology set out a challenge to act; we've taken up that charge and now we pass it along to you.

References

Alexander, K., & Day, M. (1991). *Discipline-based art education: A curriculum sampler.* Los Angeles: J. Paul Getty Museum.

Ayers, W., & Quinn, T. (2005). Series foreword. In G. Michie, *See you when we get there: Teaching for change in urban schools,* vii–ix. New York: Teachers College Press.

Blandy, D. (1994). Assuming responsibility: Disability rights and the preparation of art educators. *Studies in Art Education, 35*(3), 179–187.

Blandy, D. (1999). A disability aesthetic, inclusion, and art education. In A. Nyman and A. Jenkins (Eds.), *Issues and approaches to art students with special needs*, Reston, VA: National Art Education Association.

Bourriaud, N. (2002). *Relational aesthetics*. Dijon, France: Les Presses du réel.

Brooks, G. (1968/2005). The Chicago Picasso. *The essential Gwendolyn Brooks*, p. 91. E. Alexander (Ed.). New York: Library of America.

Brooks, G. (1987). Boy Breaking Glass. *Blacks*. Chicago: Third World Press. Retrieved on June 9, 2011 from www.poetryfoundation.org/poem/172094

Cahan, S., & Kocur, Z. (1996). *Contemporary art and multicultural education*. New York: Routledge.

Collins, G., & Sandell, R. (Eds.). (1996). *Gender issues in art education: Content, contexts, and strategies*. Reston, VA: National Art Education Association.

Cortez, J. (1996). *Somewhere in advance of nowhere*. London: Serpent's Tail.

Desai, D. (2003). Multicultural art education and the heterosexual imagination: A question of culture. *Studies in Art Education, 44*(2), 147–161.

Dewey, J. (1934). *Art as experience*. New York: Minton, Balch, & Company.

Dewhurst, M. (2010). An inevitable question: Exploring the defining features of social justice art education. *Art Education, 63*(5), 6–14.

Disu, J. (2008). This is a movement. On *The beautiful grind* (LP). Chicago: forevermaroonpublishing, ASCAP.

Douglass, F. (1987). *My bondage and my freedom*. W. L. Andrews (Ed.). Urbana: University of Illinois Press. (Original work published 1855.)

Fraser, N. (1997). *Justice interruptus: Critical reflections on the "postsocialist" condition*. New York: Routledge.

Freedman, K. (1994). About the issue: The social reconstruction of art education. *Studies in Art Education, 35*(3), 131–134.

Gaudelius, Y., & Speirs, P. (2002). *Contemporary issues in art education*. Upper Saddle River, NJ: Prentice Hall.

Greene, M. (1995). *Releasing the imagination: Essays on education, the arts, and social change*. San Francisco: Jossey-Bass.

Hicks, L. E. (1994). Social reconstruction and community. *Studies in Art Education, 35*(3), 149–156.

Holloway, D., & Krensky, B. (2001). Introduction: The arts, urban education, and social change. *Education and Urban Society, 33*(4), 354–365.

Hyde, L. (2010). *Common as air: Revolution, art and ownership*. New York: Farrar, Straus and Giroux.

Lampela, L., & Check, E. (Eds.) (2003). *From our voices: Art educators and artists speak out about lesbian, gay, bisexual and transgendered issues*. Dubuque, IA: Kendall/Hunt.

New Museum. (2010). *Rethinking contemporary art and multicultural education* (2nd ed.). New York: Routledge.

Quinn, T. (2006). Out of cite, out of mind: Social justice and art education. *The Journal of Social Theory in Art Education, 26*, 282–301.

Rogoff, I. (2010). Turning. In P. O'Neil & M. Wilson (Eds.), *Curating and the Educational Turn*. London: Open Editions.

Stuhr, P. L. (1994). Multicultural art education and social reconstruction. *Studies in Art Education, 35*(3), 171–178.

Young, I. M. (1990). *Justice and the politics of difference*. Princeton, NJ: Princeton University Press.

PART I
The Commons

Redistribution of Resources and Power

INTRODUCTION

Yours as Much as Mine

Therese Quinn

At the end of the nineteenth century, Ellen Gates Starr and Jane Addams joined together in Chicago to found the city's first settlement house. Hull-House, with classes and clubs, gymnasium and library, gallery and labor museum, and the women and men who lived in its buildings and shared ideas, energy, and a nightly meal in its dining hall, was an important manifestation of our impulse toward collectivity. Together, Hull-House residents were a force for reform. In particular, women, who would not gain the vote for another three decades, used Hull-House as a base for independent and collaborative living and organizing; their resources were jointly held and used to support common goals and goods. For example, they established the city's first kindergarten and the nation's first juvenile court, and were integral to the establishment of social work as a profession. They also called for neighborhood libraries, created parks and playgrounds, fought for child labor laws and compulsory education, and lobbied, picketed, and were arrested for workers' rights.

    The accomplishments of these activists were varied, but a way to describe the heart of their endeavor is a belief that everyone has both the possibility and the right to create and to live with beauty. Starr perhaps expressed this idea most clearly through her life's focuses; a socialist who thought that art was integral to a democratic society, she studied bookbinding in England—and is seen in the picture overleaf holding one of her books—and taught the craft and art history at Hull-House. Yet she also believed that arts education and practice was inextricable from social justice concerns, writing that, "a real and persistent love of doing good and beautiful work must, in itself, tend to bring about the conditions of doing it" (1902, p. 84).[1] Hull-House is an apt example, then, to open this section of the book, which raises questions and explores ideas about the richness and radical potential of viewing the arts as a cultural commons, and of arts education as a site of work for social justice.

Ellen Gates Starr, 1900

Walt Whitman worked and reworked two ideas in his poem, *Song of Myself*, that support this section's core contentions; these are that each of us is "immortal and fathomless" and that all of us are also *in common* with each other—"every atom belonging to me as good belongs to you." These ideas lay the ground for a way of thinking about art education that invites all people into the category of artist. It goes like this: we are unique and we share everything. The commons is the public cultural terrain where we dream, create and pass it all on. Whitman again:

> These are really the thoughts of all men in all ages and lands, they
>   are not original with me,
> If they are not yours as much as mine they are nothing, or next to
>   nothing,
> If they are not the riddle and the untying of the riddle they are
>   nothing,
> If they are not just as close as they are distant they are nothing.
> This is the grass that grows wherever the land is and the water is,
> This the common air that bathes the globe.

In this lyric Walt Whitman articulates the claim for an art that is as freely available as the grass and air, tree and flower, and blood and touch.

In support of this ideal for art education, you will find here essays about distributed art practices (David Darts on Justseeds), visual (Kevin Tavin on Heidi Cody) and aural (K. Wayne Yang on Kutiman), cultural gleanings, transborder commentaries on labor and identity (Nato Thompson on ToroLab), collaborative galaxies of self (Romi Crawford on Mequitta Ahuja), expressions of daily and ongoing containments (Edie Pistolesi on Emily Jacir), migration and memory (Kryssi Staikidis on Paula Nicho Cúmez), and records and erasures of militarism (Nicolas Lampert on Rafael Trelles). The section also includes writings about exhibitry and social movements (Doug Blandy), an arts-based critique of current education as "homework" (Dipti Desai and Elizabeth Koch), and the challenges posed by social media (Robert W. Sweeny and Hannah Johnston). We offer you these writings and images as a contribution to the commons.

Note

1 I wish to credit Sarah Anne Alford here, in whose wonderful Master's thesis, titled "Bound and Determined: Ellen Gates Starr and the Arts and Craft Movement" (2008, School of the Art Institute of Chicago), I was alerted to this quote.

References

Starr, E. (1902). The renaissance of handicraft. *International Socialist Review*, 2, 570–574.
Whitman, W. (1855). Song of myself. Retrieved August 7, 2011 from www.poetry foundation.org/poem/174745

1

JUSTSEEDS

An Artists' Cooperative

David Darts

Justseeds Artists' Cooperative might be best described as an ongoing artistic experiment. Or perhaps a shared idea realized through social action and collective creation. In practical terms, Justseeds can be understood as a decentralized network of artists working collaboratively and alongside one another, and also a DIY distribution system for socially engaged artworks like the *Cut & Paint* series.

Originally distributed in zine form,[1] *Cut & Paint* included copylefted stencil designs and a how-to guide for safely using these templates in a number of settings. The prints themselves are produced in a street art style that taps into the energy and rich history of creative cultural activism, including the anarchist, anti-war, feminist, and anti-capitalism movements. These works would look equally at home painted on a protest sign, stenciled on a sidewalk, or printed and mounted in a gallery exhibition. Engaging a host of issues from war and violence to sustainable development and consumer culture, these stencil prints demonstrate through their elegant simplicity the power of artworks to catalyze social exchange and debate and inspire critical reflection.

Justseeds was founded in 1998 by artist, curator, and social activist Josh MacPhee and began as a platform for distributing and selling politically driven artworks, including a series of posters designed to reveal and celebrate the hidden histories of human and civil rights struggles. Entitled *Celebrate People's History!*, these works produced by over 80 artists highlight individuals and groups that have contributed to the struggle for social justice and freedom but have been erased by dominant interpretations and tellings of history.

Building on the success of *Celebrate People's History!* and other related projects (see Plate 1), Justseeds evolved into a conduit for creative resistance and artistic collaboration. In 2007, MacPhee formally transformed Justseeds into a worker-owned cooperative of 26 artists where members promote each other's work,

Justseeds 7

Janet Attard/cutandpaint.org (stencil, 2004–2007)

Sue Simensky Bietila/cutandpaint.org (stencil, 2004–2007)

Sarah Healey/cutandpaint.org (stencil, 2004–2007)

Icky A./cutandpaint.org (stencil, 2004–2007)

Andalusia/cutandpaint.org (stencil, 2004–2007)

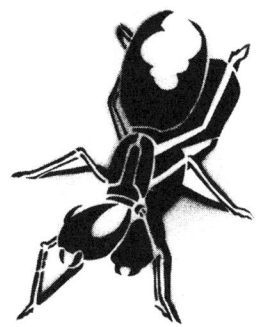

Roger Peet/cutandpaint.org (stencil, 2004–2007)

collaborate on projects, and provide ongoing support for one another. Today the group operates an online art store,[2] a collaborative blog[3] focusing on current art and creative activism projects around the world, and a small gallery space in Pittsburgh, PA.

While Justseeds describes itself as "a loose collection of creative individuals with unique viewpoints and working methods,"[4] clearly one of the defining features of the group is a deeply felt commitment to public engagement and social justice. Justseeds artists strive to reveal racial, sexual, and class-based inequities, expose concealed institutional and political power, and creatively challenge and reimagine the status quo through their work. By introducing students to Justseeds artists and artworks, art teachers can demonstrate how contemporary artists provide insights into important social and political issues and can model artful forms of civic engagement. The *Cut & Paint* series, for instance, can provide a valuable vocabulary for participating in and responding to our contemporary culture—one that could ultimately be used in the art classroom to help place young people and their artworks directly in dialogue with social issues and their communities.

Notes

1. The stencils can be downloaded from www.cutandpaint.org/
2. See http://justseeds.org/
3. See http://justseeds.org/blog/
4. See http://justseeds.org/about/who_we_are.html

2

HEIDI CODY

Letters to the World and the ABCs of Visual Culture

Kevin Tavin

One day, while teaching art education students, I drew a line down the center of the chalkboard, and asked participants to list on one side the artists that they learned about in their K-12 education. Students recalled no more than 12 artists and struggled to describe the relevance of the art to their own lives. On the other half of the board the class listed as many relevant commercial images as they could recall from childhood. Students jumped to their feet and drew images, sang aloud advertisement jingles and television theme songs, and reminisced about specific episodes and products. The classroom came alive in a unique way, as students shared experiences with toys, breakfast cereal and food packages, and advertisements. I then asked my students where dominant sites for learning reside—inside or outside of school. After some discussion and debate, most agreed that a majority of learning takes place through corporate visual culture.

Heidi Cody's *American Alphabet* (2000) (see Plate 2) speaks to this reality. *American Alphabet* spells out the alphabet with each bright and colorful letter from A through Z appropriated from a logo or brand name. From the laundry detergent *All*, to *Pez* candies, to *Zest* soap, Cody literally spells out how pervasive and recognizable images are from corporate visual culture. *American Alphabet* has been displayed in galleries through aluminum light boxes and is widely available through posters and prints. Ironically, Cody's work has recently been made more popular by being displayed as decorative art on the Bravo television series, *9 by Design*.

Cody's work, however, is more than an attractive display of appropriated corporate letters. It can also be seen as a letter to the world—a plea to recognize how commercial symbols transcend the status of mere signifiers and enter into our social imaginary. The work invites art educators to be critically attentive to visual cultural influences around us, pointing out (as my students knew very well) that individual experiences are often hemmed in by the ubiquitous and implicit threads of corporate culture. In this sense, *American Alphabet* may help raise questions about what it means to be a citizen in a world shaped and molded by consumerism, and how art education might enhance society when democracy is so often tied to consumption. Beyond recognizing the effects of visual culture on the U.S., teachers might investigate global capitalism, to challenge real life issues around the world and in local environments, such as working conditions and labor practices.

Furthermore, Cody's work raises important issues about the boundaries between art and consumerism. What questions arise, for example, when *American Alphabet* is owned and displayed by corporations, based on the visual appeal of Cody's inventive detouring of commercial graphics? How might subversive art function when used as designer eye candy on a television show celebrating capitalism? Regardless of the response, Cody's work helps us to recognize that the letters we write to ourselves about the world are already written with the letters from the world of corporate visual culture.

3

KUTIMAN

It's the Mother of All Funk Chords

K. Wayne Yang

Kutiman forages through YouTube and assembles a massive orchestra out of user-uploaded performances. The effect feels like improvisation, like a global jam session taking place in my own apartment.

"Let's just pick the mother of all funk chords," one man suggests from his corner of the screen (see Plate 3). In response, DIY webcast musicians worldwide seem to extemporize: online instructors vamp their guitars, a boy blows an arpeggio through his trumpet, a school band blares and blats while waiting in a hallway. Some are the melody: a girl breathes a haunting hook into the camera. A sidewalk lyricist lets his rhymes flow. And some are the beat: a string quartet bows two notes, and then repeats. Again and again, a girl walks to a piano and bears her fingers down on its keys. It's like watching a waterfall on endless loop, in reverse.

These are simple yet stirring moments, modestly profound in their everyday eclecticism. Kutiman weaves them into a complex polyphony. They blend so perfectly, I wonder if the momma of funk chords is actually a common human harmony, heard in shuffling shoes on subways, in lullabies, in the tappings of spoons or sticks, and if you press close enough—in the murmurs of a pumping heart?

Ever the teacher, I start to muse, how can *my* students do this? It's not as simple as making a montage from bits of movies on YouTube. Try to sample people's images without reproducing racist, misogynist, and heterosexist stereotypes! Given how we are marked—raced and gendered—such videography risks making a voyeuristic fetish film, or slightly less bad, a multicultural musical tour. Instead, Kutiman's clippings evince the players' complex personhood in a few mere seconds. Pieces of motion, scraps of time, they hint at worlds and lives behind the notes. They are not frozen portraits; they are not ethnographic spectacles; they don't claim to know too much about other people and their cultures.

Kutiman, screen-shot from *The Mother of All Funk Chords, ThruYOU*, 2009, digital video mash-up

It would make an excellent challenge for students: make your own band from found material on YouTube, but don't exploit your band members.

Since YouTube exploded in 2005, it's been a mash-up of democratic rhetoric and consumerist privilege. On one hand, YouTube might let you say something transgressive. If state censorship is evidence of radicalism, then YouTube is notable for getting blocked by Libya, Pakistan, Turkey, Thailand, Iran, Morocco, China, and nearly every public-school district in the United States. The Peabody Awards hyperbolically dubbed it a "'Speakers Corner' . . . an ever-expanding archive-cum-bulletin board that both embodies and promotes democracy." On the other hand, Google, who owns YouTube, owns everything that you say: ". . . *you hereby grant YouTube a worldwide, non-exclusive, royalty-free, sublicenseable and transferable license to use, reproduce, distribute, prepare derivative works of, display, and perform the User Submissions* . . ." Meaning your "voice" can be sampled and sold. The profit possibilities ignited copyright wars with Viacom, Universal Music Group, and other conglomerates. It's a commons owned by the corporation, a public made possible by capitalism and simultaneously a democracy made impossible by it. Kutiman toes the limits of the corporate commons too—he's a beat bandit who only steals what is unlicensed.

But as our aural and optical fields get saturated with conglomerate glib gloss, Kutiman reminds us that inventive sounds still whisper and shout, and they sound great, and they are made thru-you.

4
TOROLAB
Border Research Gone Molecular

Nato Thompson

ToroLab is a Tijuana-based collective studio and research organization whose work in a variety of media focuses on issues of migration, subsistence, and a wide variety of urban conditions. Founded in 1995, their research-based practice has gradually shifted from focusing specifically on the U.S./Mexico border region toward numerous corollaries across the globe. Their choice of aesthetic shifts according to their specific political focus, a method of working that continues to grow among activist and pedagogically oriented artists. At times, their projects appear as experimental geographic studies focused on agriculture or trans-border migration. In other instances, their work manifests as temporary architectural interventions or clothing lines that demonstrate the fragility and nomadic qualities of border existence. What holds their complex working method together (if such a requirement is at all necessary) is the constant focus on the conditions of subsistence for people living in geographies of precarity. Their consistent political curiosity allows their work to move from questions of transient architecture to those of food production and energy.

For the first ten years of the collective's existence, they predominantly focused on the Tijuana region in which they were situated. Their founding came one year after the emergence of the North American Free Trade Agreement and the ensuing conditions of neoliberal austerity measures, which were to radically alter the conditions of everyday life in their border city and became an ongoing subject of interest. In studying the phenomenon of mobility across the border for not only commercial goods, but also of people, ToroLab produced a series of studies and tactical interventions. Their *Arquitectura de Emergencia* project (see Plate 4) came out of an interest in the precarious conditions of architecture found in Tijuana. Many of Tijuana's inhabitants live as a symbiotic corollary to their cross-town neighbor of San Diego. While the U.S. builds and wastes, the emergency architecture of the border region must recycle and subsist.

ToroLab, 1995, *COMA*, 2006, ink on pencil

In amplifying and considering this lived political condition, the collective produces a tactical architecture whose qualities emphasize the need for mobility, camouflage, and re-use. *The Individual Survival Unit (S.O.S.)* provides ToroLab developed a clothing line, *Torrovestimenta*, which enabled the wearer to engage in the shifting identities and roles necessary for trans-border commuting. As an embodied form of sculpture, the clothing participates both symbolically and practically in demonstrating the specific geopolitical conditions and how they act upon a specific individual. For example, a pair of pants comes equipped with mutable pockets that hold passports and a laser visa if the wearer is Mexican, or credit cards and IDs if the wearer is American.

ToroLab are not alone in their performative investigative process that treads a fine line between aesthetic and political research. This interdisciplinary aesthetic takes as one of its fundamental qualities a belief in both participation and lived engagement with the conditions it studies. Rarely separated from the urban conditions they interrogate (in particular those of trans-border regions), their projects engage and make palpable the political realities of their research. This form of interrogation, while certainly lacking a convenient discursive home (is this art, geography, education, all of them or none?), provides a lens from which to catch a glimpse of aesthetic pedagogic forms on the horizon.

ized a moment within the Blue Sky Project residency of 2007.

5

MEQUITTA AHUJA

Afrogalaxy

Romi Crawford

> I have often wondered why the farthest-out position always feels right to me.[1]

In *Zami: A New Spelling of My Name* (1982) the writer Audre Lorde solves the riddle of her own identity by claiming a writing form, "biomythography," that allows her to draw on multiple dimensions, the facts as well as the imaginings and fictions, of her persona. The aim was to create "a new literary genre, empowered by feminism, that exploded male-centered definitions of history, mythology, autobiography and fiction."[2] In effect, she mines from a decisive ideological stance, the "farthest-out position," to generate a new sense and representation of self that "feels right" to her. She positions herself on the outer reaches, towards the darker matter, of her identity in order to take in a better perspective—of a pliable and open, rather than a fixed and resolute self.

Artist Mequitta Ahuja actively refers to Lorde's concept of "biomythography" to make paintings that interject aspects of a communal or shared history, personal mythologies, and the social imaginary into the discourse of self portraiture. She describes *Afrogalaxy* (2007) (see Plate 5) as an "automythography collaborative." While the painting starts with a photograph that she takes of herself, the end result, an enamel on paper rendering of an exuberant Afro-shaped orb that seems to weigh down the bent torso of a finely costumed figure, is in fact a group effort.

Ahuja, the founding Program Designer and Director of the Blue Sky Project, worked with a group of eight teenagers, who served as co-collaborators on the work. Operational since 2005, The Blue Sky Project is an eight-week artist residency with the goal of bringing two disparate factions together, professional artists and Dayton, Ohio teenagers, in the making of contemporary art. Artists such as Ahuja are open to an extreme manner of experimentation and risk as they attempt to make work that incorporates the creative impulses and suggestions of an unknown youth cohort.

For Ahuja, a well-positioned artist, praised for her painterly abilities, who has a recognizable aesthetic, and who is known for her assertion of ethnic/racial motifs (such as hair and costuming), to reposition herself and her practice, each summer at The Blue Sky Project, suggests the best type of ecological smartness. Ahuja's project encourages us to consider how we can activate renewed interpretations of our work. This in turn helps us towards having renewed interpretations of our communities, our world, and even ourselves.

We live in a moment of smart houses and design, aesthetics that try to take into account the preservation of our world. Yet, projects such as *Afrogalaxy* point to the possibility of generating new creative forms and modalities that force us into alternate positions, which reallocate the normative terms of creative/scholarly authority. We educators, artists, and citizens, are responsible for generating these new forms, programs, and platforms that will bring us into strange and unexpected relations with one another. This facilitates our "feeling right" about others within the galaxy and it helps us to "feel right" about ourselves.

Notes

1 Audre Lorde, *Zami: A New Spelling of My Name—A Biomythography* (The Crossing Press, 1982), 15.
2 Darryl L. Wellington, *The Crisis*, March/April 2004.

6

EMILY JACIR

The Intersection of Art and Politics

Edie Pistolesi

"Nakba," or catastrophe, is the name given for Israel's 1948 ethnic cleansing of Palestinians, a process that has continued to the present. International human rights organizations have repeatedly condemned Israel's brutal attacks, including the destruction of Palestinian towns, some describing it as gradual genocide. Worldwide protests surged after the 2009 "Operation Cast Lead" Israeli attack of Gaza, and again with the May 31, 2010 assault of the Gaza aid flotilla in international waters. Israel's bombardment of schools, hospitals, ambulances, and United Nations facilities has resulted in injuries and deaths of thousands of civilians, many of them children. Israel continues its ethnic cleansing of the Palestinian population through the destruction of homes and crops, and the withholding of food, water, and medical supplies.

This is the political backdrop of artist Emily Jacir, a Palestinian American who lives in New York and Palestine, and works at the intersection of art and politics. Jacir is an activist artist whose work addresses the plight of the Palestinian people through universal themes of home and community. The theme of home is also about being homeless. In her work titled *Memorial to 418 Palestinian Villages which were Destroyed, Depopulated and Occupied by Israel in 1948* (see Plate 6), Jacir created a canvas refugee tent containing the names of 418 villages where Palestinians were marched away from their homes to lives of refugee status. The tent is shaped like a house but is not a house. It is temporary shelter for people who cannot go home. Jacir created the piece while working in New York, where names of the destroyed villages were hand stitched onto the tent with black thread by 140 volunteers. The act of hand sewing is meditative painstaking work; especially when sewing on heavy canvas. The stitching of each village name is part of a collective act of remembering and grieving for people who lived in that place that was taken from them.

Go to my mother's grave in Jerusalem on her birthday and put flowers and pray.

I need permission to go to Jerusalem. On the occasion of my mother's birthday, I was denied an entry permit.

- Munir
Born in Jerusalem, living in Bethlehem
Palestinian Passport and West Bank I.D.
Father and Mother from Jerusalem
(both exiled in 1948)

Notes: When I reached the grave of his mother, I was surprised to see a circle of tourists surrounding a grave nearby. It was the grave of Oskar Schindler...buried next to a woman whose son living a few kilometers away is forbidden paying his respects without a permit. There were many graves that had smashed crosses and sculptures of the Virgin Mary destroyed. The caretaker of the cemetary told me that Jewish extremists had raided the cemetary and desecrated many of the graves. He showed me the ones he fixed.

زوري قبر والدتي يوم عيد ميلادها و ضعي الورود على قبرها و صلي.

كنت بحاجة إلى تصريح للذهاب إلى القدس في يوم عيد ميلاد و الدتي، و لكن تم رفض منحي التصريح.

- منير
من مواليد بيت لحم، و يعيش في بيت لحم
جواز سفر فلسطيني/هوية ضفة غربية
الأب و الأم من القدس
(نفيا عام ١٩٤٨)

ملاحظات: عندما وصلت قبر والدته فوجئت بمجموعة من السياح يحيطون بقبر قريب. كان ذلك قبر أوسكار شندلر. الرجل الذي يرقد الآن بجوار السيدة التي لا يستطيع ولدها الحي، لزيارتها بدون الحصول على تصريح. و الذي يقيم بضعة كيلو مترات فقط. لقد وجدت العديد من الصلبان و تماثيل السيدة مريم العذراء محطمة. قال لي حارس المقبرة إن مجموعة من اليهود المتعصبين هاجموا المقبرة والطوا المزار بالعديد من القبور. لقد أراني الحارس الصلبان و التماثيل التي أعادها إلى مواضعها.

Emily Jacir, *Where We Come From,* 2001–2003, detail *(Munir)*
American passport, 30 texts, 32 c-prints and 1 video
Text *(Munir)*: 9½ × 11½ in./24 × 29 cm

Photo *(Munir)*: 35 × 27 in./89 × 68.5 cm

When speaking with people who live in tragic circumstances, it takes commitment to go beyond words of sympathy and ask, "What can I do?" Emily Jacir asked that question to exiled Palestinians. Their answers, fulfilled by Jacir, were documented in the installation, *Where We Come From*. Because Jacir is an American citizen, her U.S. passport allowed her to go where exiled Palestinians could not; to their old neighborhoods in Palestine that they called home. The wishes of the exiled were for the small acts of daily life. "Drink the water in my parents' village." "Go to my mother's grave in Jerusalem on her birthday and place flowers and pray." The photographs and documentation of Jacir's actions in *Where We Come From*, interactively allow us to go with her and bear witness to mundane actions that become precious ceremonies as each one is carried out.

Emily Jacir's artwork reveals to viewers the universal plight of human beings who suffer the loss of home and homeland. Their wishes and dreams are the wishes and dreams of everybody, and their heartbreaking sense of loss becomes ours as well.

7

PAULA NICHO CÚMEZ

Crossing Borders

Kryssi Staikidis

Paula Nicho Cúmez speaks from the heart about immigrant rights, the breaking up of beloved families and what it must feel like to be forced to leave that which you love, all that you know, and your home. Through our work together, and the closeness of a mentorship where I became Paula's student, friend, and colleague, Paula gave me a glimpse into her reality. Paula describes her painting *Crossing Borders* (see Plate 7):

> Why do I title this *Crossing Borders?* There are many people who have been forced to travel to other parts of the world, or who perhaps desire happiness, or another life for their families in another land. Unfortunately, I have seen many people leave, and sometimes people triumph, and sometimes they fail. In this painting, we see the little dog crying, howling, because that's how things go when someone leaves their place of birth. Most of what we feel is the pain of the families who are left behind. I am reminded of all who have left, suffering, to find a good job.

In *Crossing Borders*, a Maya Kaqchikel woman is dressed in traditional *traje* wearing a *huipil*, a woven tunic. The woman is flying, a repeated theme in Paula's work, which indicates the success of women. She is with her back to us, her wings spread, her anonymity assured. Because her face is hidden from view, she might be any indigenous person forced to leave home. In this picture, the woman's dog is bidding her a sad goodbye as she leaves her homeland, crossing borders. Here the sadness of the dog becomes a metaphor for the results of the injustice of exploitation that forces, in this case, an indigenous woman, to leave her cherished home and migrate in order to survive.

Paula Nicho Cúmez 23

Paula Nicho Cúmez, *Cánto a la Naturaleza* (Song to Nature), 2005, 24 × 32 in.

In conversations I had with Paula about her work, she conveyed her desire for all who saw it to know about her pride in her Maya Kaqchikel culture and her belief in the importance of holding on to the traditions of her culture for future generations. In this painting, Paula addresses the need for crossing borders because of the difficult social and economic conditions facing indigenous communities in Guatemala, due in part to a brutal military dictatorship that slaughtered Maya communities, killing 200,000 people with U.S. support during the years 1962–1996 (Kiernan, 2007).

Concepts of social justice such as equality for all indigenous peoples and the hope of a non-violent society are threaded throughout Paula's work as she represents the strength of Maya traditions, traditional clothing, and the importance of women in Maya communities. Each component of her painting serves a purpose that is integrally linked with culture, its celebration and preservation. Constantly aware of the need to protect her culture and her people, Paula's work reflects her vision, which seeks a world without borders, where recognition of the beauty of indigenous cultures is restored.

References

Kiernan, B. (2007). *Blood and soil: A world history of genocide and extermination from Sparta to Darfur.* New Haven: Yale University Press.

8

RAFAEL TRELLES

Cleaning Up the Stain of Militarism

Nicolas Lampert

The rebellion and underground edge of the modern day street art movement has faded. Born out of New York City in the 1970s and 1980s, artists—mostly disenfranchised black, brown, and white youth—bombed the trains, subway tunnels, and walls of the city and launched a global phenomenon. The explosive colors and designs screamed out against power, privilege, and property. Today, street art has gone mainstream. Corporations hire street artists to paint billboard advertisements. Street artists have their own merchandise lines with mass-produced T-shirts, hoodies, and skateboards that are churned out of the sweatshops of China and the global south. Shepard Fairey's images can be seen wheat pasted all over Pittsburgh . . . to promote his museum show at the Warhol. In the U.K., workers employed to clean up graffiti by Network Rail are instructed not to remove Banksy's stencils because it might negatively impact tourism.

Lost in the new rules of the street art career path and individual branding is dissent and social justice. The atypical street artist is the political street artist whose motivation derives from the urgent need to communicate political messages to the public through images and text. Rafael Trelles, a Puerto Rican interdisciplinary artist, represents this vital sub-subgenre.

Trelles's street art medium is reverse stencils—environmental street art where he creates images by *cleaning*. Spray paint and its toxic legacy are avoided. Instead, specific areas of dirt and built-up layers of pollution are removed from a wall with a power washer to produce a design that stands out against the areas of the surface that remains untouched.

Trelles's venture into reverse stencils began a decade ago. His iconic street art image is of a dove breaking a warplane (see Plate 8), an image that condemns the U.S. Navy's practice of turning the island of Vieques into a bombing range. His image and technique becomes metaphoric. Cleaning the walls to clean up

Rafael Trelles, *Helicopter and Butterflies*, 2005, water-washed concrete

society. Cleaning the walls to cleanse the stain of war, militarism, and imperialism. Cleaning the walls to help kick the U.S. Navy off Vieques, a victory that was achieved in 2003 after a long protest movement.

Trelles's street art becomes so vital for it is part of a local and international movement that calls for justice. Equally important, his work is part of the environmental street art movement. Yet, we should be mindful that it is the imagery and the intent of the artist that matters, for environmental street art has also been co-opted. Today, a growing number of "environmental" advertising firms (Green Graffiti, Mind the Curb, Element Six Media, etc.) hire street artists and offer a range of services that places corporate logos and messages on sidewalks, walls, and other surfaces with eco-friendly materials. All of which equates to green capitalism and little to no systemic changes. Luckily, we can turn to Trelles for inspiration as an artist who keeps it real, an artist who harnesses environmental art for grassroots organizing and social justice movements, instead of corporate profits.

9

EXPERIENCE, DISCOVER, INTERPRET, AND COMMUNICATE

Material Culture Studies and Social Justice in Art Education

Doug Blandy

In early May 2010 a Spanish/English ceremony dedicated the *Northgate Peace and Forgiveness Garden* in Salem, Oregon. This garden of flowers and raised vegetable beds is dedicated to the memory of Montez Bailey. Bailey, along with two of his friends, was shot in the Northgate Park in 2009. Bailey died of his wounds. The alleged assailants fled to Mexico and are currently facing extradition. Northgate residents see the *Peace and Forgiveness Garden* as both a memorial to Bailey and a community-based effort to take back the park from gang activity. The park bench where Bailey was shot is now located at the home of his parents in northeast Salem. Written on the bench are messages about Bailey. This garden, coupled with the park bench, have become emblematic of efforts by residents of northeast Salem to build community and restore a sense of place to a neighborhood marked by violence. Emblematic of social justice movements is the material culture they generate—in this case a garden and bench. Also consider the lunch counter and the Civil Rights Movement, the wheelchair and the Disability Rights Movement, Rosie the Riveter and the Feminist Movement, and the folk music associated with the Anti-War Movement during the 1960s among many examples that could be cited.

Bolin and I (2003) define material culture as:

> All human-mediated sights, sounds, smells, tastes, objects, forms, and expressions ... When there is purposeful human intervention, based on cultural activity, there is material culture. This being the case, nothing affected by human agency is overlooked as too insignificant for intensive examination, nor viewed as too small for eliciting substantive meaning.

(p. 250)

Northgate Peace and Forgiveness Garden, 2010, Salem, Oregon

Given this definition, the material culture associated with social justice will include, but not be limited to, works of art, music, ritual, dress, movement, theater, multi-media, time-based media, textual documentation, slogans, buttons, and oral histories. Together this material culture supports solidarity within a movement while simultaneously communicating the values, attitudes, and beliefs of the movement to those outside. For these reasons fully understanding and appreciating a social justice movement is only possible by engaging with the material culture associated with it. Interestingly, given the importance of such material to social justice movements, such material has not been widely studied (Reed, 2010).

Using the example of the *Northgate Peace and Forgiveness Garden*, my purpose in this chapter is to discuss strategies through which students and teachers can engage with social movements through the study of the material culture associated with them. Readers should bring to this chapter their own knowledge of the material culture of social justice movements that they have been a part of or are aware of. I will delineate the steps associated with doing "fieldwork" as a way of discovering the material associated with a social justice movement. Interpreting fieldwork so that emphasis is placed on the possibility of ongoing collaboration with the community being interpreted as well as those who will experience the interpretation will be emphasized. I will also describe a participatory curatorial approach that teachers and students can use in communicating their study and immersion in communities formed around a social justice purpose while simultaneously identifying the material culture that supports a community's efforts to promote social justice.

Experience and Discover

A first step in understanding and appreciating material culture such as the *Northgate Peace and Forgiveness Garden* is to experience it systemically. Becker's (1984) systemic conceptualization of "art worlds" can be helpful in this regard. Art worlds, much like social movements, are defined by the people, organizations, institutions, and assorted other entities that as a network facilitate and support the creation, distribution, and appreciation of a work of art. Becker uses the term "art" broadly and it includes, but is not limited to, the material created by fine artists, folk artists, craftspeople, media specialists, as well as the way that we embellish and amplify what we do in our everyday lives.

Students can use research methods informed by anthropology and folklore to discover the larger systems that material culture, like the *Northgate Peace and Forgiveness Garden*, operate within. Lassiter's (2004) collaborative ethnography is particularly useful in this regard. Lassiter promotes collaborative ethnography as one way to try and achieve a correct interpretation, representation, or description of a cultural group and the material culture it produces.

Lassiter's method includes the following:

1. participating in the lives of others (which may include learning a new language or learning how to behave appropriately within a particular setting);
2. observing behavior (which may include that of the ethnographer herself as well as that of the community);
3. taking field notes (which may include jotting down first impressions, drawing maps, or writing extensive descriptions of cultural scenes); and
4. conducting interviews (which may include both informal conversations and more formal exchanges).

(p. 2)

Students studying the *Northgate Peace and Forgiveness Garden* using collaborative ethnography would examine the history of northeast Salem and the history of Latinos in Salem, identify social institutions (churches, social service organizations, government agencies, schools) serving the area, interview people associated with such institutions, identify informal networks existing within the community, interview people associated with those networks, spend time in the *Northgate Peace and Forgiveness Garden*, talk to people in the garden, and document their experiences in the community using multiple media including text, photographs, and video.

Interpretation

Material collected through collaborative ethnography is in a raw form until it is "interpreted." It is through interpretation that people will develop an emotional and intellectual response to the material (National Association of Interpretation, 2009). Interpretation occurs through a variety of media including, but not limited to, film, video, text, audio, photographs, theatrical re-enactments, websites, and mobile device apps among other means of communication.

Lassiter (2004) emphasizes that in representing and interpreting others, a first responsibility is to those who are being represented and interpreted. These individuals should be intimately involved as consultants in all aspects of the program. Interpretation that is ethical will have the consent of those being interpreted involve those being studied in the interpretive process. Students should be able to articulate to others the reasons for their interest in a particular situation, the educational institution they are associated with, and speak to their fieldwork and interpretive methods. If cultural property is involved the legal rights of those associated with this property must be respected and appropriate recognition made (Kurin, 1997).

Welsh (2005) conceptualized several approaches to interpretation that can guide students in their analysis and communication of the material collected about acts of social justice and are both congruent with a collaborative ethnographic approach and best ethical practices. Based on Welsh's typology of interpretation, students should be encouraged to allow for self-representation by those studied to the greatest extent possible. Questions like the following, associated with the *Northgate Peace and Forgiveness Garden*, suggest how the work of Welsh can be applied. What characterizes the voices of those involved with the *Northgate Peace and Forgiveness Garden*? How can those voices be best represented? How can others be encouraged to have a stake in the information and knowledge associated with the study of the garden? How can the interpretation be transparent in practice, thus giving audiences a glimpse into how the knowledge is prepared, who is involved, and the decision-making processes of those doing the interpretation? How can multiple interpretations be cultivated in the audiences encountering the material? How can an experience with the material collected allow audiences to ask their own questions about the garden and the situation that motivated the creation of the garden? How can audiences be actively engaged with the material collected?

Communication

Curated exhibits are one of many ways in which the interpretation of material culture is made known to others. In 1986 Congdon and I developed a participatory method of exhibition design compatible with material collected and interpreted as described above. Our method requires interpreters and exhibit designers to work in partnership with community members (Blandy & Congdon, 1993). Our method is based on pedagogical guidelines from Freire (1970, 1981) that focus on building non-hierarchical and cooperative relationships among people, methods for critical inquiry, the importance of forging a common language, and a conception of culture and community that is dynamic. Our method facilitates non-hierarchical relationships among interpreters, exhibit designers, and community members. In the case of the *Northgate Peace and Forgiveness Garden*, members of the community who could be involved in the process would include gardeners, family members, volunteers, object holders, government workers, social service workers and members of the police among others. Our curatorial method consists of six overlapping and dynamic phases of activity. These phases include:

1. Orientation
Problems and questions are posed by the primary facilitators regarding the context for the exhibit and appropriate research strategies for investigating the problems and who, what, where, when, why, and how questions. For example:

- How can a specific community practice be best represented in the exhibit?
- Who from the community can assist in planning the exhibit?

- When is it appropriate or not appropriate to share with the general public a community practice?
- What interpretive strategies will be used?

2. Identification of partners
Problems and questions are posed regarding key partners in planning and implementing the exhibit are identified. Problems and questions address, but are not limited to, development of shared language, clarification of exhibit purpose and roles of various partners.

3. Planning
Problems and questions are posed regarding the process of deciding what is to be included in the exhibit.

4. Implementation
Problems and questions are posed regarding the identification of key participants in the implementation process and decisions about the logistics of making the exhibit available to the public.

5. The Exhibit Occurs
Interpretation and installation are congruent with phases 1, 2, 3, 4, and 6. Interpretation and installation are congruent with the values, attitudes, and beliefs of community members and best practices in exhibit installation and interpretation.

6. Evaluation
Problems and questions are posed regarding the identification of appropriate qualitative and/or quantitative evaluation strategies regarding all aspects of the planning and implementation of the exhibit.

In the case of the *Northgate Peace and Forgiveness Garden* I can imagine an exhibit that would include historical and contemporary photographs and snapshots of the neighborhood, news reports of the shootings, testimonials about the impact of the shootings on family and community members, documentation about how the community came together to plan and implement the garden, and documentation around the everyday life of the garden. Ideally such an exhibit would occur in the neighborhood of the garden and be paired with public programming that would further amplify the neighborhood, the socio-cultural context in which this neighborhood exists and the garden. I can imagine an exhibit that would be participatory in that it could include an interactive website or some other type of communications space where community members and the general public could post additional comments about the neighborhood, Bailey's death, and the resulting garden.

Conclusion

Fully understanding and appreciating a social justice movement is only possible by engaging with the material culture associated with it. Using the example of the *Northgate Peace and Forgiveness Garden* I have recommended strategies through which students and teachers can engage with social movements through the study of the material culture associated with them. These strategies, associated with experience and discovery, interpretation, and curation, are grounded in ethical practice and will assist students and teachers in engaging with historical and contemporary social justice movements associated with their communities.

References

Becker, H. S. (1984). *Art worlds*. Berkeley, CA: University of California.

Blandy, D., & Congdon, K. G. (1993). A theoretical structure for educational partnerships and curatorial practices. *Visual Arts Research*, *19*(2), 61–67.

Bolin, P. E., & Blandy, D. (2003). Beyond visual culture: Seven statements of support for material culture studies in art education. *Studies in Art Education*, *44*(3), 246–263.

Freire, P. (1970). *Pedagogy of the oppressed*. New York, NY: Seabury.

Freire, P. (1981). *Education for critical consciousness*. New York, NY: Continuum.

Kurin, R. (1997). *Reflections of a culture broker*. Washington, DC: Smithsonian.

Lassiter, L. E. (2004). Collaborative ethnography. *Anthronotes*, *25*(1), 1–9.

National Association for Interpretation. (2009). *Standards and practices for interpretation*. Retrieved August 9, 2011 from www.interpnet.com/download/BP-Methods-Jan09.pdf

Reed, T. V. *Social movements and culture*. Retrieved September 12, 2010 from http://culturalpolitics.net/social_movements

Welsh, P. H. (2005). Re-configuring museums. *Museum Management and Curatorship*, *20*, 103–130.

10
EDUCATIONAL CRISIS
An Artistic Intervention

Dipti Desai and Elizabeth Koch

Dipti Desai

I ask my art education students at New York University, "What do you want your students to remember about art 50 years from now?" In other words, what notion of art would you like to insert into public memory? These questions encourage deep thinking about the role of art, artists, and education in our democratic society. It is precisely these kinds of questions that have recently come under attack by the media, educational policy makers, and conservatives. For example David Steiner, commissioner for the New York State Department of Education, recently speaking about teacher preparation claimed that "colleges still devote too much class time to abstract notions about 'the role of school in democracy'" and "the view by some that schools exist to perpetuate a social hierarchy" (quoted in Foderaro, 2010, para. 9).

One of the significant challenges of our times is the current move to construct education as an enterprise that calls for standardization, accountability, and corporatization of pedagogy. Several artists have taken on the idea of pedagogy by making art production itself a site of study (including 16 Beaver Group, Rainer Ganahl, Alex Villar, Fritz Haeg, and Elizabeth Koch, whose work is discussed later in this chapter). Their artworks explore what it means to learn and ways of rethinking how knowledge is produced in schools. By designing educational exchanges that engage in alternative methods of teaching and learning, these art practices are examples of what Gayatri Spivak (1993) has called "unlearning." These artistic practices, I suggest, are one possible avenue of rethinking education as a cultural–aesthetic practice that is engaged in the redefinition of knowledge. In this essay, I explore a collaborative piece called *Homework* that provokes dialogue about how the space called education is produced in our society. The work calls

Elizabeth Koch, *Watch and Learn (Or Not!)*, May 2010, iMovie shown on MacBook

into question the ways the corporatization of education in schools and universities has shifted the terrain of education from a social good to a market-driven, strictly professional endeavor that is about outcomes and transferable knowledge. This global shift in education, dominated by what Irit Rogoff (2010) calls "economies of cognitive capitalism," is working in tandem with the unprecedented politicization of education as Steiner's earlier quote makes apparent.

Homework, created by the collaborative team of Ditte Lyngkaer Pedersen, Carlos Motta, Lize Mogel, and Jeuno JE Kim, is conceived simultaneously as a study group, editorial team, and curatorial collaborative. Their work investigates the relationship between art, education, and politics. Questioning our understanding of education as a neutral practice, *Homework* is a site of investigation, debate, dialogue, and dissent. As a creative political project, it "is based on processes, where each homework is a self-initiated assignment to practice [a] continuous critical engagement with notions of the 'political'" (para. 5). The artistic collaborative team met in person only twice in 2007, however every Tuesday they used Skype as their classroom for discussing what "political" means in visual arts and education. Their dialogue was shared with a larger audience through the web-zine called artwurl.org, a project of PS 122 gallery in New York City (http://interfacekultur.au.dk/fileadmin/www.interfacekultur.au.dk/motta.pdf).

Their curriculum is based on an investigation of the terms "political" and "pedagogy." As they indicate:

> by implementing a "school" structure, *Homework* is constructed to emulate a knowledge colony, whose members serve as both teachers and students, where each participant conducts and applies various research models to understand better the idea of the "political" and what it means to be politically engaged cultural producer.
>
> *(para. 6)*

One of the essential questions in their curriculum is: what is being "produced, discussed and censored in the arts" (para. 6). Each "lesson" then interrogates the idea of how our understanding of what we consider as art is shaped in particular ways by the field of art education. By asking the questions what does it mean to make art that is political, they are not only challenging the neutrality of art, but also asking us to think about the kind of artworks we produce in art classes given the dominance of images that are canonized and co-opted by the market economy. I believe that *Homework* is an educational space where "learning how to unlearn and what to unlearn" (Spivak quoted in Danius & Jonsson, 1993, p. 24) become central concepts, providing an example of rethinking curricula and lessons in art education. Each unlearning then opens possibilities of new unlearning as one's subject position changes with each unlearning. As a generative process then the structure of their exploration cannot be a pre-determined product and is solely process oriented. This learning process that produces knowledge that has to be continually questioned, makes visible "knowledge as struggle" (Rogoff, 2010, para. 17).

Homework explores the intersection of art and education outside of the "traditional instruments of learning" (Spivak quoted in Danius & Jonsson, 1993, p. 25). So, what does it mean for art educators working within schools to examine the notion of education? The installation *Cracked* by Elizabeth Koch is one example of the kinds of exploration regarding K–12 pedagogy that can take place in schools. Similar to *Homework*, *Cracked* questions the structures, apparatuses, skills, and techniques that discipline art and education by focusing on the current testing environment that governs all curricula in schools. By asking students, teachers and the general public what education should look like in schools, the installation foregrounds the redistribution of resources and curricula shifts that needs to take place in our society.

What can we learn from these educational sites in art? It is evident that we need to envision our classrooms as fluid spaces that allow for the exploration of divergent views by experimenting with different methods of representation in and outside schools. The power of the image to enact change can no longer be taken for granted given the canonization and co-optation of images by the media and market. This means we need to begin the process of unlearning what we have learnt about art/image as both teachers and students. This unlearning allows us to imagine alternative ways of teaching and learning in art education, which again cannot be taken for granted, always needing to be questioned.

Elizabeth Koch

As a student in the Art Education program at New York University, I was regularly asked to think about the relationship between art education and democracy. My professor Dipti Desai helped me question if my curricula perpetuated the systems of dominance already in place in the U.S. or if it encouraged students to think deeply about the world around them, their role in it, and the ways they could create change. I personally make every effort to run a democratic classroom, where sharing ideas and experiential thinking is valued. However, the standardized testing movement is eating away at the precious time that I have with my students.

The installation *Cracked* emerged out of my experiences as a current school teacher in a 4th grade class at a public school in New York City. It addressed the purpose of education in our society and raised questions about what it means to learn and how learning is affected by politics. The ideas for *Cracked* emerged out of frustration about both the time lost to preparation for standardized tests and the unnecessary pressure that tests place on young students. The installation was composed of a school desk covered with chewing gum and text, silver-framed text about teaching and learning, and a video of my students taking the 4th grade standardized test that is interspaced with a survey conducted among students, teachers and the larger public about their views on the purpose of education.

The gum desk, entitled *Ode to Lost Enthusiasm*, was a collaboration with students in the 4th grade. Every day of test prep, students received gum to chew and afterwards they would put it on the desk. This small form of rebellion brought so much pleasure to the students and it was my way to speak back to the pressures of The No Child Left Behind Act experienced by teachers on the culture of their classrooms.

Our school day runs from 8:20 am to 3:10 pm. That equates to 6 hours and 50 minutes of school a day. Of that time, students spend 1 hour and 35 minutes out of the classroom at lunch, recess, and a specials class (art, music, physical education). Which means students have 5 hours and 15 minutes of class a day, adding up to 26 hours and 15 minutes in class a week. During that time, teachers are expected to cover math, reading, writing, grammar, spelling, science, social studies, handwriting, and geography. These are the subjects mandated by the New York State Department of Education and the Board of Education in the city. How to best teach these required subject's to students is a constant debate among "experts" in the field of education, and is now determined by educational policy makers based on notions of job training, transference of knowledge, and skills for the market economy. High-stakes testing is part of free-market capitalism and has also become a political tool.

I used a public survey as the entry point for my art installation. I wanted to know what students, parents, and the general public think about the purpose of education. I distributed a hundred images of a brain and asked people to write down what they felt children should learn in elementary school. Using this information, I created a video that contrasts the reality of preparing for standardized tests with the public's notion of an ideal educational experience. Although the survey was mixed regarding the way to educate elementary students, not one person thought that test taking was a crucial and necessary life skill. I juxtaposed the survey with comments I thought were important, such as: learning is an active process; follow your passion; ask questions until you understand; be world citizens. The kids' views on what to learn in school were to get along with other kids, to write cool stories, poetry, science experiments, reading, fashion design, and the general public's views on education were to dream big; to tap into your creative side; the art of physically writing; true history with an emphasis on women and minorities; and science is an art. I placed these comments with the images of students taking the 4th grade national test. The students' body language indicated stress, discomfort, and anxiety.

My installation is the culmination of a project-based approach to education that I believe is an alternative that still provides the skills for a market-driven society, but it also allows students to learn to connect different subjects by posing questions that they investigate, learn about ethics, values and beliefs, cooperation, and relationally as a core aspect of social relations in an unequally structured society. Some of the benefits of project-based learning include: building a strong sense of community through common experiences, learning in a real world context so that students see that they can do things that have an impact on the world in which they live, learning about reflection and drafting through peer, teacher and expert critiques, and engaging fully in the inquiry process from problem to solution (Berger, 2003).

This approach does not mean that we should not give our students tests or that memorization is not a useful skill, but rather that teaching needs to be experienced within the context of learning about subjects with real meaning to young people. To pose questions, to debate, and to allow students to form their own opinions about issues that are important to them cannot be reduced to a test-driven education shaped to serve the free-market economy.

References

Berger, R. (2003). *An ethic of excellence: Building a culture of craftsmanship with students.* Portsmouth, NH: Heinemann.

Danius, S., & Jonsson, S. (1993). An interview with Gayatri Chakrovorty Spivak. *Boundary 2, 20*(2).

Foderaro, L. W. (2010). Alternate path for teachers gains ground. *New York Times.* Retrieved on June 6, 2010 from www.nytimes.com/2010/04/19/education/19regents.html

Rogoff, I. (2010). Free, *e-Flux Journal #14*, retrieved on June 13, 2010 from www.e-flux.com/journal/view/120

Spivak, G. (1993). *Outside in the teaching machine.* New York: Routledge.

11

SOCIAL MEDIA/SOCIAL JUSTICE

The (Creative) Commons
and K-12 Art Education

Robert W. Sweeny and Hannah Johnston

Rem(a)inder

Overnight, the signs appeared. Crudely made and displayed, they consisted of simple elements that added up to a confusing product. Or did not add up, the declarative statement and the silhouetted form irreducible to a clear conclusion. They existed in tension, between themselves and the space, between the object and the subject. "The War is Over."

The work of Freewayblogger (Freewayblogger.com) serves as a reminder of the war in Iraq, still being waged at the time of this writing, seven years after then-President Bush declared "mission accomplished" (CNN, 2003). It reminds the viewer that the victim of torture at Abu Ghraib (Hersh, 2004) depicted in the image has still not been identified. This work also serves as a remainder, an additional symbol that does not fit neatly into the political narratives associated with the War on Terror. The phrase and the image remain; the war is not over, and the human being represented in stark black and white still stands, a visualization of the reluctance of the U.S. government to renounce torture and close spaces where rendition occurs, such as the so-called "black sites" located around the globe, as well as Guantanamo Bay.

This work remains long after it has been torn from the chain-link fencing above the LA freeway where it was first displayed. It exists as reproduction, on the Freewayblogger.com site, and on the cameraphones of intrigued passersby. It exists in the space of the commons, where public dialogue is generated through interaction and dissent, through verbal, visual, and physical means. It is a reminder of the productive capabilities of the human body, the *biopower* that torture seeks to redirect or silence (Foucault, 1976). It is the relationship between the body and social media that the authors will explore in this chapter, through brief

Freewayblogger, *The War is Over*, 2004–2008, interventions on California freeways, dimensions variable

discussions of artists engaged in explorations of social media, politics, race, class, and corporate power.

Blackness for Sale

> This heirloom has been in the possession of the seller for twenty-eight years. Mr. Obadike's Blackness has been used primarily in the United States and its functionality outside of the US cannot be guaranteed. Buyer will receive a certificate of authenticity.

The new media work of Keith and Mendi Obadike deals with numerous topics, the most prominent of which is the relationship between race and new media art itself. *Blackness for Sale* (2001) uses the online auction site *eBay* to raise questions about the commodification of race and the possibilities for artistic intervention in the spaces of digital consumerism. It challenges the space itself; as quoted above, the buyer receives a "certificate of authenticity," but no other physical property changes hands. However, the project did attract individuals willing to purchase this "item." As the artists write: "[A]fter four days, eBay closed the auction due to the 'inappropriateness' of the item. [A]fter 12 bids, his blackness reached its peak at $152.50" (Obadike, 2001).

This project outlines possibilities for artistic intervention in the spaces of social media, through a project that speaks in part to the history of the slave trade in the U.S., where skin color was equated with humanness. The Obadikes invert this interpretation, commodifying the self. Additionally, what becomes commodified in the process is the reputation of the individual buyer and seller; the relationship between this reputation and cultural signifiers such as race are illuminated through *Blackness for Sale*.

If *The War is Over* acts to remind the viewer about the impact of the War on Terror on the bodies of those tortured at Abu Ghraib and those driving on freeways in machines that use the main export of the war-torn region, *Blackness for Sale* removes the body from the discussion. This disembodiment is common in discussions of new media works of art, particularly those that use the Internet, a space in which traditional signifiers are destabilized. However, as Nakamura (2006) points out, these signifiers are still present; in fact, as the space of electronic interaction incorporates commercial exchange, race may become one of the aspects of identity available to the highest bidder in the spaces of digital commerce.

Skin

> Writer Shelly Jackson invites participants in a new work entitled "Skin." Each participant must agree to have one word of the story tattooed upon his or her body.
>
> *(Jackson, 2003)*

Shelly Jackson is an author perhaps best known for her hypertext novel *Patchwork Girl* (1995). This novel utilizes electronic media to piece together the parts of a female protagonist, constructing narratives that are open-ended and in flux. For her 2003 project *Skin*, Jackson asked volunteers to tattoo one word from her story on their bodies, rethinking the digital traditions of hypertext while maintaining her interest in fragmentary bodies and narratives.

Skin re-envisions literature as it challenges the ownership of cultural forms of production; in this case, using the body as medium. Jackson claims to hold all rights to the "work," which she promises not to reproduce liberally. It is not clear, however, how this ownership relates to the body of another. In this manner, she plays creatively with notions of public and private space, body and art, developing a participatory text in and through the contemporary commons.

Each of the artworks that have been discussed previously relates to contemporary social media and the body through access to what is termed the "commons." As Hardt and Negri (2009) discuss, the commons is both physical and transactional, and is always political. In this conversation, it should be thought of as the ways in which individuals conflict and create in shared spaces. In these examples, the commons entails interactions that are multifaceted: Freewayblogger questions issues of reproducibility and free speech through the shared space of the freeway overpass; the Obadikes explore the exchange value of race in the electronic marketplace; Shelly Jackson asks participants to mark their bodies with her words, claiming ownership over the text that is a collection of bodies.

The artistic, social, and legal challenges represented in part by social media have resulted in the Creative Commons (CC), which was established in 2001 with support of The Center for the Public Domain (Creative Commons, 2010). Under CC, the creator maintains the ability to determine how creative works can be used, marking a dramatic shift in traditions of copyright. The relationship between the body and CC in the works discussed previously relates to what Foucault (1976) termed *biopower*. Biopower relates to the ability for individuals to produce and control power framed in such a way that opens up possibilities neglected in past formulations of social, political, and economic power. Each individual has the ability to expend this power as she or he sees fit, though conglomerations of administrative might threaten to divert this energy at every turn.

The spaces of art education have always consisted of intersections between bodies and power, between the individual and the group, and between the ephemeral and the physical. Art education traditionally deals in the production of physical objects through immaterial (educational) means. Art educators have the opportunity to address issues related to the body and creative expression, making physical the ephemeral interactions related to social media, and perhaps, more importantly, dematerializing the physical production that runs through many art educational traditions.

The goal in heightening awareness of these ideas is to bring them into art educational spaces in order that students understand social media in art and society at large. If art students are to think critically and engage resourcefully and with social relevance, then they must critically process and respond to current media. We propose that art educators look at the core elements underlying the sphere of social media to design lessons for the classroom which address observed changes in art and society through studio production and discussion. Creating lessons that translate and interpret the changes in social media into traditional media rather than simply replicating the use of social media will bring students to a more thorough understanding of the relationship between society and identity, corporations and the individual.

"Cropped Identity"

A friend from China apologized for falling out of contact for a few months. She said that Facebook had been banned by the government to pressure the social media hub into removing posted information that tainted China's reputation. As soon as the information was removed, Facebook was re-opened to the public. The page "owner" has a sense of individual power, but, as seen in Jackson's *Skin* (2003), power is always nested. When related to biopower, both the page "owner" and the tattoo "owner" operate in complex networks of legal, social, and personal exchange.

Social media provides individuals with a means of editing, filtering, or cropping to create an augmented version of individual identity, whether in the form of a blogspot, avatar, Wikipedia page or Facebook profile. In the privacy of personal technology, a person selects his/her own photos and individually determines which bits of information to reveal about him/herself. Details about gender, marital status, age and even interests are edited by the individual. The creator chooses how he or she will be viewed. In contrast to private diaries, blogs, by their very nature of being accessible to all, force an automatic filtering system that shapes what is presented on the page.

Wiki spaces and Wikipedia give multiple individuals the ability to add, crop and edit information presented. In this context, a collaborative, or *networked*, identity is developed and the information is in flux (Sweeny, 2009). On Facebook, others contribute comments, pictures and wall posts that add to the individually created identity.

With regard to biopower and identity, Marshall (1996) states: "technologies of domination act essentially on the body, and classify and objectify individuals . . . in technologies of the self there is the belief now common in western culture, that it is possible to reveal the truth about one's self." To explore the relationship between identity and social media, students must first be brought into a conversation about this notion of truth, providing a foundation for understanding, responding to and communicating the concept of "cropped identity."

Social Media and Social Justice?

Each of these suggestions represents opportunities for art educators to respond to contemporary challenges generated through the use of social media. Issues of political activism, racial identity, and individuality have been highlighted, though they are by no means the only issues being raised by contemporary artists using social media. Central to each of these examples is the changing notion of the body in relation to technologies that are closely tied to notions of impermanence and ephemerality. Art educators operate at the intersection where the physical and the ephemeral cross, where the immaterial labor of education results in material productivity. Art educators who are invested in issues of social justice should explore inversions of these binaries: what might the material product of the ephemeral process of education—the conversations, border crossings, and arguments—look like? How might a creative commons approach to curriculum design change the investment and engagement of those participating in the educational process? How might artists living in an age of social media respond to issues of identity fragmentation and corporate influence? What would an immaterial art education look like? The biopower of each and every individual, linked through complex social media networks, represents vast possibilities for the construction of a collaborative, critical, creative commons.

References

CNN (2003). *Commander in chief lands on USS Lincoln*. Accessed 6/10 from www.cnn.com/2003/ALLPOLITICS/05/01/bush.carrier.landing/

Creative Commons (2010). *About Creative Commons*. Accessed 6/10 from http://creativecommons.org/about

Foucault, M. (1976). *Discipline and punish*. New York, NY: Pantheon.

Hardt, M, & Negri, A. (2009). *Commonwealth*. Cambridge, MA: Belnap Press of Harvard University Press.

Hersh, S. (2004). Torture at Abu Ghraib. *New Yorker Magazine*. Accessed 6/10 from www.newyorker.com/archive/2004/05/10/040510fa_fact

Jackson, S. (1995). *Patchwork girl*. Watertown, MA: Eastgate Systems.

Jackson, S. (2003). *Skin* [work of art]. Accessed 6/10 from http://ineradicablestain.com/skin.html

Marshall, J. (1996). Education in the mode of information: Some philosophical considerations. *Philosophy of Education*. Accessed 9/10 from www.ed.uiuc.edu/EPS/PES-yearbook/96_docs/marshall.html#fnB1

Nakamura, L. (2006). *Race in cyberspace: Visual cultures of the Internet*. Minneapolis, MN: University of Minnesota Press.

Obadike, K. & M. (2001), *Blackness for sale*. Accessed 6/10 from www.blacknetart.com/index1_1.html

Sweeny, R. (2009). There's no "I" in YouTube: Social media, art education and networked identity. *Journal of Education through Art*, 5(2 & 3). Bristol: Intellect Press.

PART II
Our Cultures
Recognition and Representation

INTRODUCTION

Build Something Fresh

John Ploof

> We were kids without fathers . . . so we found our fathers on wax and on the streets and in history, and in a way, that was a gift. We got to pick and choose the ancestors who would inspire the world we were going to make for ourselves . . . Our fathers were gone, usually because they just bounced, but we took their old records and used them to build something fresh.
>
> (Jay-Z, 2010, p. 255)

Building something fresh is, for hip-hop artists like Jay-Z, the requisite outcome of sampling or appropriating words or images. Anything is fair game; however, quotes can't simply be lifted. Sources need to be extended in meaningful ways, or in other words, artists must utilize that which came before them to "build something fresh," of their own making.

I know what it means to be a kid without a father. Reading Jay-Z's words, I wonder how much of our knowledge of this subject-position cuts across the spectrum and what gets lost in translation. The construction and recognition of complex social identities has often called into question the taxonomies of old school identity politics, categories that have sometimes worked to essentialize difference. Hall (1996) stated that identity as a concept has been "operating 'under erasure' in the interval between reversal and emergence; an idea which cannot be thought in the old way, but without which certain key questions cannot be thought at all" (p. 2). Recent epistemological viewpoints may afford us useful ways of valuing our histories while recognizing the limitations of how we had previously conceptualized them. "Scholarly and activist projects that mobilize politicized identities in the service of social justice point to new horizons, as well as mapping the limits of identity politics" (Mohanty, 2010, p. 538). What if we were to take these old records and, considering the litany of critiques, use them to build something fresh?

The Vogue Evolution dance crew is from New York City. The members of Vogue Evolution are Dashaun Williams, Devon Webster, Malechi Williams, Leiomy Maldonado, and Jorel Rios

All Under Construction

Remixing recognition relies on critically considering our relational perspectives—based on socially constructed histories of difference, belonging, and emerging futures—all under construction. Opening this section is Carrie Sandahl's essay on the work of Kaisa Leka, a Finnish artist whose cartoon drawings explore the social meanings of (dis)ability paired with "spirituality, sexuality, and politics ... along with the shape of her feet." Dónal O'Donoghue's essay considers the "organization and normalization of gender and sexuality in American society," in and through the narrative textile work of Darrel Morris. Anne-Marie Tupuola centralizes her own cultural perspective alongside that of artist Nicholas Galanin, whose sculptural work delves into commodified portrayals of his indigenous culture to jam with futures that are "urban, politicized and cosmopolitan." Dalida María Benfield's essay on Kimsooja's installation and performance work articulates the layers and connections that shape and reshape the politics of a shared world against the "insistent and industrialized production of cultural difference."

Civil Drawings

Buzz Spector's examination of artist Xu Bing's work reveals that Bing's printed texts resemble Chinese calligraphy; however, they are instead a constructed hybrid language that appears "Chinese on the outside and English on the inside," and unreadable in traditional ways by anyone fluent in these languages. James Haywood Rolling, Jr. interprets the cutout symbols of Bernard Williams' installations as "layers of an archaeological dig," that can be explored, though the associative meanings brought by readers to understand and contribute to "the evolving identity of our nation as a living text." Hock E Aye Vi Edgar Heap of Birds' site-specific signage spells out the words, "The Fighting Illini" in backwards type. Elizabeth Delacruz characterizes this act of reversing type as an interventionist strategy developed by Heap of Birds that calls us to critically reread the history of the University of Illinois from that of a public land grant university, to that of land taken from native peoples. Samuel Fosso's self-portraits are viewed through the lens of queer studies, as "performances of realness," by G. E. Washington. Here, vogue dance competitions are aptly referenced to conjure a definition of realness that equates with, "convincingly passing as someone else while creatively presenting your identity."

A World for Ourselves

Links between theory and practice are explored in the next section, through three chapters that illuminate issues of recognition and representation in teaching and learning contexts. Olivia Gude examines the culture and pedagogy of the Spiral Workshop, a project that involves teens in the development of thematically sequenced curriculum. Spiral's quirky themes generate relational inquiry rather than simply representing or illustrating that which is already known. Miia Collanus and Tiina Heinonen articulate their experiences of a program for future textile teachers at the University of Helsinki, Finland. They identify a dichotomy of theory and practice in craft education and call for a shift to a critical paradigm for educating about the socio-cultural context of craft. Korina Jocson brings her research interests in literacy and youth cultural studies to an interview with artist and teacher Brett Cook. Their conversation addresses issues of recognition and representation that exist within the reality of our world; however, on a fundamental level, they also defy categorization and that which we already know.

This complex process of identifying and simultaneously defying may, in fact, help us get closer to what Muñoz (2009) recognized "as necessary modes of stepping-out of this place and time to something fuller, vaster, more sensual, and brighter" (p. 189). In the following pages, contributors to this section call us to consider our lives as more brilliant and expansive than yet imagined.

References

Hall, S. (1996). Introduction: Who needs "identity"? In S. Hall & P. du Gay (Eds.), *Questions of Cultural Identity* (pp. 1–17), London: Sage.

Jay-Z. (2010). *Decoded*. New York: Spiegel & Grau.

Mohanty, C. T. (2010). Social justice and the politics of identity. In M. Wetherell & C. T. Mohanty (Eds.), *The Sage Handbook of Identities* (pp. 529–539), London: Sage.

Muñoz, J. E. (2009). *Cruising utopia: The then and there of queer futurity*. New York: New York University Press.

12
KAISA LEKA
Confusing the Disability/Ability Divide

Carrie Sandahl

Finnish artist Kaisa Leka can be considered a member of the growing international disability arts and culture movement. Across the globe, disabled people are recognizing that their unique bodies are vital sources of creative generation and knowledge, not to be hidden away under lap blankets or put away in institutions. Leka's autobiographical graphic novel, *I Am Not These Feet* (see Plate 9), is a complicated entry in the growing collection of work by disabled artists whose stories of claiming disability reject and complicate the tired, simplistic tales of "overcoming," "inspiration," or "tragedy." Leka's diary chronicles her decision to become, in a sense, more disabled—to have her deformed and arthritic feet amputated and replaced with high-tech prosthetic limbs. She becomes more "able" because of disability as her prostheses offer her more mobility and less pain. The diary takes us through her decision-making process, her hospitalization experience, and her discovery of life as a differently *disabled* person.

She communicates this complexity using a starkly simple aesthetic of black and white cartoon drawings in a scant 60 or so pages. Most of her characters are cartoon mice (reminiscent of Disney's early Mickey Mouse) differentiated from one another only by a prop or piece of clothing. The complexity arises not from the drawings, then, but from Leka's narrative structure. She layers straightforward narration with exposition interrupted by personal asides to the reader. In so doing, she constantly revises and splinters her story, throwing what we know at any point in the story into doubt. She presents to the reader both a public brave face and a private ironic, wickedly funny, and slightly neurotic face at the same time. The text itself retains an aesthetic of imperfection and revision. The diary retains crossed-out misspellings, revisions, and arrows to correct her English word order.

Though Leka asserts "I am not my feet," the entire novel reveals how she is who she is because of her feet. Her feet have informed every aspect of her being

Kaisa Leka, *I Get Excited*, 2003, from *I Am Not These Feet*, Absolute Truth Press

from her gender identity and body image to her experiences of pain (that do not completely go away after the surgery) and her acute perception of ableism in the world around her. Her spirituality, sexuality, and politics all take shape along with the shape of her feet. The reader, then, must constantly reassess what she means by her claim *not* to be her feet. Her assertion cannot be interpreted through simplistic platitudes those of us with disabilities hear throughout our lives, that we are beautiful on the "inside," where it counts, as if our outsides are informed by disability but the inside is not. Her feet belong to who she is; her inside self cannot be separated from her outside self. Whether her feet are there in the flesh or whether they have been replaced by prosthetics, Leka's feet have an important story to tell.

13

DARREL MORRIS

Men Don't Sew in Public

Dónal O'Donoghue

Men Don't Sew in Public: Made in the USA is an appliqué and embroidered soft sculpture made by the Kentucky-born artist, Darrel Morris. Best known for his small hand-made textile panels featuring men and boys (many of which are autobiographical), in this work Morris continues his inquiry into the organization and normalization of gender and sexuality in American society. He produces a piece that challenges and destabilizes deeply rooted expectations of what men should do in public. The work serves as an example of how masculine identity and male subjectivity is constituted in and through processes of negative differentiation. This topic has engaged Morris for many years; he has created an extended body of work that seeks to problematize common-sense notions about men, masculinity, and sexuality (see Plate 10).

While this artwork directs attention to something we take for granted, and serves as a reminder that work practices continue to be delineated by gender and constituted by particular understandings of gender, it prompts us to consider the gendered realities and lived experiences of men in the U.S. in this century. Specifically, it directs attention to ways in which gender gets constituted in, and through acts that are possible in specific social contexts and social conventions. Judith Butler (2006) reminds us, and this work renders visible, that "there are social contexts and conventions within which certain acts not only become possible but become conceivable as acts at all" (p. 66). Men sewing in public is an act that we never encounter, and therefore raises the question, what are the gender codes that do not allow men to sew in public?

For Morris, who grew up in a coal-mining community, learning to sew, braid, and quilt from his grandmother, Pearl Morris, was a transgressive act. In that transgressive spirit, in this artwork he presents the declarative statement, "men don't sew in public," which, at first, appears to be a claim to an authentic and

Darrel Morris, *Cushion #3*, 2000, cotton perle, canvas, Poly-Fil, 6½ × 6 ½ × 3 in.

traditional masculine identity informed by a belief in universalism and essentialism. However, the statement actually works to destabilize the very gender order it proclaims. In doing so, the work invites several alternative statements and scenarios, such as "Men Sew in Public"; these suggest new possibilities for men to live differently.

In this work, meaning is suggested and embedded in the materials that Morris used, and in his making processes—sewing, felting, embroidering, and appliquéing. Morris's artwork and art practice teach us that art making is a rich site where issues about living and life can be investigated, interrogated and given form. This work sets the conditions where new and difficult questions can and must be asked about men, masculinity, and sexuality. *Men Don't Sew in Public: Made in the USA* reminds us that nothing is fixed, and things can be otherwise.

References

Butler, J. (2006). Performative acts and gender constitution: An essay in phenomenology and feminist theory. In M. Arnot & M. Mac an Ghaill (Eds.). *The Routledge Falmer Reader in Gender and Education*, London: Routledge, pp. 61–71.

14

NICHOLAS GALANIN

Imaginary Indian and the Indigenous Gaze

Anne-Marie Tupuola

As media and public discourse embrace post-colonial and post-racial hype, the cost to affected cultures and communities is often ignored. Publicly, it is increasingly cool to be ethnic and to claim an indigenous[1] identity, yet, privately, indigenous peoples are struggling to own and direct their scripts. I am a woman of Samoan descent living in an era where the colonial perspective, in theory, is in decline. My own multi-media work seeks to reverse the colonized gaze[2] of the Polynesian female commonly associated with the alluring and sexualized dusky maiden and the primitive noble savage. The politics of representation are therefore my daily reality. My identity script must compete with popular and misappropriate stereotypes of the "authentic" Polynesian woman and the increasing commodification of my culture.

In his provocative installation *Imaginary Indian* (see Plate 11), Nicholas Galanin, born in Sitka Alaska, captures the misrepresentation of aboriginal cultures. His choice of materials and images turns the exploitation of such cultures on its head. On a backdrop of toile wallpaper are miniature figures frolicking across pastoral landscapes. On the front hang a variety of tribal objects and masks of the northwest coast, similar to those commodified and exploited for the sake of the tourist dollar. Interestingly, customary hangings are camouflaged by the same toile wallpaper, possibly to re-appropriate the indigenous gaze and highlight the fluidity of aboriginal identities. The deliberate location of both European and traditional materials hallmarks a shift in the indigenous discourse from submissiveness towards empowerment. The *Imaginary Indian* installation is thus a timely challenge for the observer to view indigenous identities through a panoramic lens. The term "Imaginary Indian" seems to suggest that it is not the aboriginal peoples who are at odds with their identity. Rather, it is the imaginary and, in essence, commodified portrayal of their cultures that is out of touch and in need of revision.

60 Anne-Marie Tupuola

Nicholas Galanin, detail image from *Imaginary Indian* series, 2009, wood, paint, wallpaper

Re-appropriating native cultures is also important to Galanin's work as a young aboriginal hip-hop artist. In this predominantly Americanized genre he uses traditional aboriginal music and dance movements as a way of celebrating and acknowledging contemporary and fluid indigenous identities. A similar form of hip-hop can be found in the works of some Maori and Pacific youth in Aotearoa/ New Zealand whereby greater emphasis on customary music, images and lyrics legitimizes and lifts the visibility of indigenous languages. In essence, through hip-hop the portrayal of native identities is shifting from one that is primitive towards one that is urban, politicized and cosmopolitan.

Indigenous art is a valuable platform for exposing the cultural and political tensions that underscore the representation of indigenous cultures. Galanin's *Imaginary Indian* illustrates the potential to view aboriginal identities within an imaginary context. However, it is his use and position of materials that empower and call for indigenous peoples to actively reverse the colonial gaze back to the indigenous where it belongs.

Notes

1 Here, indigenous refers to "native" and aboriginal peoples of a country, including their contemporary and customary arts, identities and languages.
2 Analysis and interpretation are through a colonially biased lens that is often stereotypical and ethnocentric.

15

KIMSOOJA

The Performance of Universality

Dalida María Benfield

Kimsooja is a video, installation, and performance artist who makes site-specific interventions, often with her own body as the intervening material. Through her visually layered and process-intensive work, experiences of time and space, history and geo-political location, are disentangled and reshaped with a novel sense of human connectedness. This instantiates a form of universality, a practice of being with others that suggests a more just and humane society. Across various contexts—political, geographical and cultural—she puts her body in relation to other bodies. She stands on the line separating the local and the global, spectator and spectacle, and her body opens onto the social body. She captures and holds time, which allows the making of this path. As the artist writes about her works, "They have in common universality, a timelessness that encapsulates both past and present" (2010b, para 4).

These acts of connection occur in diverse times and spaces. The video work *A Needle Woman* (1999–2000) consists of images of the artist standing amid crowds of people in different cities across the globe. This work enables, with some effort, a recognition of the artist's body, yet it simultaneously effects an erasure of that body, a disappearance of her in the crowd. As we come to recognize her stillness, a sharp contrast is elicited between the artist's body and her environment of moving bodies, creating a sense of temporal and spatial vertigo. The artist's body, as she encapsulates a space of non-movement, becomes a vehicle towards another dimension. Recognition and erasure, appearance and disappearance, alongside "timelessness," constitute the threshold upon which Kimsooja's work rests.

Mumbai: A Laundry Field (2010a) (see Plate 12) is an artwork of temporal and spatial phases: a series of performances, a series of photographs, an installation of video screens. While each of these gestures unfolds with its own logic, each returns us to an original moment; again, the artist's still body in the frame. Instead of speed and the clatter of movement, there is an arc of silence, the body making

Kimsooja, *Cities on the Move—2727 km Bottari Truck*, 2007, Giclée, print on Hahnemüele paper, 24½ × 34 in.

its own time. The "laundry field" is a tableau, a site mapped in colors and lines. Folds of many-colored fabric fall across the screen, becoming evocative inscriptions of humanity. Amid this milieu, the artist's body, covered in fabric, lies still. The traces of human labor are memorialized and materialized through the artist's body. That activity, the past, now connects us, a universality that is produced by finding this body, among the residue of others, paying close attention to the particular rhythms of the fabric.

Kimsooja's politics reimagine how we might live together, sharing a world. Her sense of universality is not one that easily fits within existing political discourses, but instead insists on an open-ended articulation of presence, the simultaneity of "past and present." It is clearly posed, however, against the insistent and industrialized production of cultural difference, which orders the world of global capitalism according to race, nation and gender. Recognition of difference might be liberatory or oppressive. Sidestepping the question of recognition, Kimsooja's work practices a form of liberatory disappearance. This is not an erasure, but an invocation, of herself and other people across cultures and places, positing connection across differences, simultaneity across sequence, and shared space across disparate spaces.

References

Kimsooja. (1999–2000). *A Needle Woman*. Performance, video and installation.
Kimsooja. (2010a). *Mumbai: A Laundry Field*. Performance, video and installation.
Kimsooja. (2010b). *Artist's Statement*. Retrieved May 12, 2010, from www.kimsooja.com.

1 Nicolas Lampert, *Learn About Black Panther Party History*, 2010, silkscreen, 19 × 25 in., image based upon a 1937 WPA/Federal Art Project poster design by Carken (full name unknown)

2 Heidi Cody, *American Alphabet*, 2000, aluminum light boxes with Lambda Duratrans prints, 28 × 28 × 10 in.

3 Kutiman, screen-shot from *The Mother of All Funk Chords*, ThruYOU, 2009, digital video mash-up

4 Torolab, 1995, *Emergency Architecture* project, "S.O.S. Emergency Architecture," 2001, digital image

5 Mequitta Ahuja with assistance from Blue Sky Project, *Afrogalaxy*, 2007, enamel on paper, 96 × 104 in.

6 Emily Jacir, *Memorial to 418 Palestinian Villages which were Destroyed, Depopulated and Occupied by Israel in 1948*, 2001. Refugee tent, embroidery thread, daily log of names of people who worked on tent; 8 × 12 × 10 ft.

7 Paula Nicho Cúmez, *Cruzando Fronteras* (Crossing Borders), 2007, 24 × 32 in.

8 Rafael Trelles working on *War Plane and Dove*, 2005, water-washed concrete

9 Kaisa Leka, Cover, 2003, *I Am Not These Feet*, Absolute Truth Press

10 Darrel Morris, *You Promised Me*, 1993, found fabric, sewing thread, canvas, 6 × 9 × 0.25 in.

11 Nicholas Galanin, *Imaginary Indian*, 2009, wood, paint, wall paper, 27 × 67 × 6 in., 52.5 × 42.5 × 11 in.

16
XU BING
Words of Art

Buzz Spector

> I collect things. After Tiananmen Square I collected a bicycle that had been crushed flat by a tank.
>
> *(Xu Bing, in a lecture at the Elvehjem Museum of Art, September 3, 2004)*

Xu Bing, born in Chongqing, China, in 1955, is one of the most influential figures among the many Chinese artists that emigrated to the West in the years just before and after the tumultuous 1989 student protests in Beijing's Tiananmen Square. Xu Bing grew up in Beijing. Like many urban Chinese youth coming of age in the days of the Cultural Revolution, Xu Bing was sent to the countryside for "re-education" in 1974. While living and working on a rural commune, he drew pictures and rendered calligraphy for a local newsletter. His precocious artistic ability gained Xu Bing admission to the Central Academy of Fine Arts (CAFA), and he returned to Beijing in 1977 to study printmaking.

During his years of study at CAFA, Xu Bing developed a uniquely personal graphic style in his woodcuts and drawings. The absence of sanctioned Socialist Realist imagery in Xu Bing's art was subtly at odds with the Chinese Communist policy that art should serve the people, but its apparently non-political subject matter was tolerated until 1989, after Xu Bing exhibited his enormous installation, *Book from the Sky* (see Plate 13), in Beijing's National Museum of Fine Arts. The installation included hundreds of printed handmade books on the floor, over which 50-foot-long printed scrolls were suspended, while the walls of the space were lined with printed panels. Xu Bing's printed texts graphically resembled Chinese calligraphy, but were in fact composed of unreadable invented characters created by the artist. *Book from the Sky* was harshly criticized by government officials for its textual meaninglessness, and the controversy helped spur Xu Bing to emigrate

Xu Bing, Practicing Square Word Calligraphy. Top: *Introduction to Square Word Calligraphy*; bottom: *Square Word Calligraphy Red Line Tracing Book*, both "standard edition," 1996, 15 × 9 in. (closed)

to the U.S., where he lived until 2008 before returning to Beijing and CAFA, where he now serves as vice president.

Xu Bing's Square Word Calligraphy extends the artist's interests in language, reading, and writing as social and communal activities. This unique linguistic hybrid is graphically structured like Chinese calligraphy, but the gestures forming its characters in fact spell out English letters. From 1994, when he first introduced the concept, to the present day, Xu Bing continues to offer instruction in writing his invented language to viewers of his art. The two books the artist produced to demonstrate his method, *Introduction to Square Word Calligraphy* and *Square Word Calligraphy Red Line Tracing Book*, have the appearance of traditional Chinese writing manuals, with text appearing in vertical columns. Since Xu Bing incorporates letter strokes like those used in actual Chinese writing, it takes some seconds of looking before viewers, whether Chinese or not, grasp the paradox of words that resemble Chinese on the outside and English on the inside, as if each language were in disguise. Amusement and appreciation quickly follow.

But Square Word Calligraphy isn't just a word game. Regardless of cultural origin, viewers who sit down to practice writing in Xu Bing's language are learning both the gestures of calligraphic expression and the importance of reading between the lines.

17

BERNARD WILLIAMS

Art as Reinterpretation, Identity as Art

James Haywood Rolling, Jr.

Bernard Williams is a collector of story fragments—stylized black cutouts and heavily outlined images of faces, costumes, weaponry, architecture, types of vehicles, household and recreational artifacts, along with signs and placards denoting ethnicities, locations, phrases and events—all culled from the annals of our national experience as if they were the layers of an archaeological dig. Espousing what he calls a "museum aesthetic," Williams does not collect in order to categorize. Rather, Williams surreptitiously raids categories and appropriates symbols, objects, images, and information in order to reinterpret and reimagine what it means to be American (see Plate 14).

Williams writes that his murals, paintings, and hieroglyphic installations are composed of "neither histories, chronologies, nor taxonomies."[1] Contrary to taxonomical structuring, which is inherently hierarchical and predictable, the art of Bernard Williams is composed of "borderland" spaces (Anzaldúa, 1988). Williams invites his audience to give up easy assumptions about who represents America to instead risk the "transformative potential of the margin" (herising, 2005, p. 144). Like the artists of the Harlem Renaissance, his work reinterprets the complex of American stories, however unpredictably.

At first glance, the hieroglyphics in Williams's work individually appear familiar. And then we become aware that we are not being asked to simultaneously unpack all meaning at once as if each work were one singular canvas. Instead, we find ourselves slowly *reading* the work as a complex lexicon of symbols that will ultimately require the support of other associative readings to fully comprehend. When interpretation is informed by the works of other artists and authors, overwritten by personal memory and experience, and guided by dialogue toward filling in any initial gaps of understanding, we truly learn as we go.

Bernard Williams 69

Bernard Williams, *Buffalo Chart*, installation view at the Art Gallery of Ontario, Canada, 2009, dimensions variable, painted wood and found objects

Like the fabled "cutting contests" of the early jazz era (a form of competitive engagement where each musician would try to out-improvise the other in a battle to shift local axes of power and prestige), the symbolic interaction of Williams's paintings and installations provides an array of opportunities for teachers and students to reconstruct the texts of American identity, while at the same time disrupting the stubborn representational power of popular cultural myths and stereotypes. In the work of Williams, symbols not only interact—his representation of Anglo, Black, Hispanic, Asian, Native American, and other U.S. identities also collide and reassemble.

Walter Truett Anderson (1997) claims that "personal identities would be hard to locate without the network of symbols within which we are defined and the internal monologue with which we continually remind ourselves who we think we are" (p. 263). The art of Bernard Williams can aid educators in fulfilling their responsibility to present the evolving identity of our nation as a living text, a work-in-progress to which our students have every right to contribute.

Note

1   See www.cpag.net/home/artistbios/williams.html.

References

Anderson, W. T. (1997). *The future of the self: Inventing the postmodern person*. New York: Tarcher/Putnam.

Anzaldúa, G. (1988). Bridges, drawbridge, sandbar, or island. In M. Blasius & S. Phelan (Eds.), *We are everywhere: A historical sourcebook of gay and lesbian politics* (pp. 712–722). New York: Routledge.

herising, F. (2005). Interrupting positions: Critical thresholds and queer pro/positions. In L. Brown & S. Strega (Eds.), *Research as resistance: Critical, indigenous, & anti-oppressive approaches* (pp. 127–151). Toronto: Canadian Scholars' Press.

18

HOCK E AYE VI EDGAR HEAP OF BIRDS

Beyond the Chief

Elizabeth Delacruz

> All republics or nation states exist as a result of acts of aggression, displacement or replacement. The nature of their creation is to eclipse or absorb previous societies and governmental groups.[1]

Cheyenne-Arapaho artist Hock E Aye Vi Edgar Heap of Birds is known for his multi-disciplinary forms of public art. These include large-scale drawings, acrylic paintings, lithograph prints, steel outdoor sculpture, and political site-specific public signage projects. The *Beyond the Chief* project (see Plate 15) was a 12-panel public art installation commemorating Indigenous peoples whose homelands are within the boundaries of the state of Illinois. In response to a National Collegiate Athletic Association (NCAA) ruling banning post-season bowl games for universities using offensive or racist team mascots, in 2007 the University of Illinois's Board of Trustees voted to end the use of the Chief Illiniwek name, image, and regalia as the official mascot of the Urbana campus. The University of Illinois retained the name "Fighting Illini" for its athletic teams. This decision was reached after over 20 years of protest and controversy over the Chief Illiniwek mascot and name "Fighting Illini." The university's continued use of the term "Fighting Illini" remains controversial.

The *Beyond the Chief* installation is a reminder from Heap of Birds that this land was never truly granted to the University of Illinois, a public land grant university, but taken from the native peoples. Heap of Birds spelled the words "The Fighting Illini" backwards, "to turn the University around, to turn the students around, to turn Illinois around."[2] According to Heap of Birds,

> It's really a memorial to the tribes that are gone. The signs are self-referential. When natives make memorials to themselves or their losses that's more important than a college mascot or other issue. Everything doesn't have to be about the dominant white culture.[3]

Hock E Aye Vi Edgar Heap of Birds, *Beyond the Chief*, a 12-panel public art installation of signage (defaced) at the University of Illinois, Urbana campus

Seven of the panels were vandalized or stolen over a five-month period between February and December 2009. According to Heap of Birds, this was the first time his art had ever been vandalized. Despite the artist's claim that each sign had a value of $10,000, the local District Attorney valued the signs at $300 and filed only misdemeanor charges against a student who was caught on police surveillance videotape removing one of the signs.

Edgar Heap of Birds' art confronts the issue of racism in America and the common practice of taking Native names and using them as team mascots and other forms of entertainment in popular culture. For Heap of Birds, such popular uses of Native imagery does not honor native Americans; rather,

> When you think about the land and you think about the community, you have to come to the politics, also, and look at those issues. And it's very difficult . . . I think it's time to change all that. It's time to really respect Native people for their own selves, not for their uses in commerce.[4,5]

Notes

1 Artist's statement in association with his work "Most Serene Republics" for the 2007 Venice Biennale project, supported by the Smithsonian's National Museum of the American Indian. See www.chgs.umn.edu/museum/responses/heapOfBirds/serene Republics/artistStatement.pdf.
2 See Brian Dolimar's summary, *Edgar Heap of Birds Speaks at Closing of "Beyond the Chief" Exhibit* at www.ucimc.org/content/edgar-heap-birds-speaks-closing-"beyond-chief"-exhibit.
3 Comments given by Heap of Birds during an interview with local newspaper reporter, Melissa Merrill. See www.news-gazette.com/news/arts-and-entertainment/art/2009-05-17/native-hosts-artist-surprised-sad-see-signs-vandalized.ht.
4 See artist's statement for the Walker Art Center in association with *Telling Many Magpies, Telling Black Wolf, Telling Hachivi* at www.walkerart.org/ace/tye/wac_sl_media/wac_hob_1c.html.
5 For additional information about art educators' roles in the Indian mascot controversy, see E. M. Delacruz "Racism American Style: Art Education's Role in the Indian Mascot Issue", published in 2003 in the journal *Art Education*, 56(3), and the National Art Education 2010 Position Statement Regarding the use of Race-Based Mascots in Educational Settings at www.arteducators.org/about-us/Position_Statement_Regarding_the_Use_of_Race_Based_Mascots_in_Educational_Settings.pdf.

19

SAMUEL FOSSO

Queering Performances of Realness

G. E. Washington

As a child Samuel Fosso was a refugee who lost his mother, fled war, and at the age of 13 secured a job as a shoemaker's assistant in the Central African Republic. By 1975, at the age of 15, he was managing his own portrait and passport studio, but he also cultivated a practice of taking formal portraits of himself. He found his own body, contemporary African culture, fashion, and politics sources of endless fascination. Knowing nothing about professional art, the teenage Fosso made photographs to send to his grandmother and future children (Mapurunga, 2009). Yet, as a curious, fearless, and self-absorbed adolescent, Fosso's pictures inhabited stories of a world he didn't know. Now as a successful international artist, he continues to situate himself in the space of the other.

Liberated American Woman of the '70s (see Plate 16)—the English translation—is the title of a colorful image of Fosso "posed" in heavy femme make-up wearing a pants suit with a fake pearl necklace, straw cowboy hat, and purple pointed-toe high heels. He is sitting on a red and white plastic tablecloth in profile but looking straight into the camera with his upper torso twisted gently to the right. Behind him is a plastic backdrop with fake green tropical plants.

Fosso's photographs as well as his artmaking process are *performances of realness*. As defined by the participants in *Paris is Burning*, Jennie Livingston's (1990) documentary on vogue dance competitions in Harlem, *realness* is convincingly passing as someone else while creatively presenting your identity. In Livingston's film and Fosso's photographs realness is a momentary attempt to defy one's social standing while presenting open, honest, and authentic plays on the possibilities of identification. This fluidity is a defining characteristic of *queer*.

Here, queer is not simply gay, and things thought to be gay are not merely queer. "Queer is not only queer; it is not identical with itself" (Pinar, 1998, p. 6). Queering is questioning convention and seeing what it is not, what is normal and what is a freakish deviation, what is ordinary and what is not (Butler, 1997). Fosso's images introduce a way of seeing that critiques the inextricable relationship between our identities—what we are and are not doing—and our behaviors.

Together Fosso's image and biography can serve as introductions to social justice in the art classroom. Like a vogue dancer, *La Femme Americaine Liberée* messes with vision, but it also provokes the viewer to ask how we might "create a world that is more just, more fair, as well as one that is more compassionate" towards the other (Risner & Stinson, 2010, p. 3). A young vogue dancer on season four of MTV's *America's Best Dance Crew* articulates keenly the queer challenge, "This is not about us. It's about what we are representing" (YouTube ABDC 4, 2009). The image that queers us is about who *we* are, not what *it* is. Like Samuel Fosso's portrait process, teachers might begin in the classroom by queerly situating our students and ourselves within the imaging of our own stories and our shared new worlds.

References

Butler, J. (1997). *Excitable speech*. New York: Routledge.
Livingston, J. (1990). *Paris is burning*. (Hollywood, CA: Miramax Film/documentary.)
Mapurunga, J. (2009). *Facing Samuel Fosso*. Universidad de Barcelona. Retrieved January 15, 2011, from http://issuu.com/mapurungando/docs/samuel_fosso_article_mapurunga.
Pinar, W.F. (1998). Introduction. In William F. Pinar (Ed.), *Queer theory in education* (pp. 1–39). London: Lawrence Erlbaum Associates, Publishers.
Risner, D., & Stinson, S.W. (2010). Moving social justice: Challenges, fears, and possibilities in dance education. *International Journal of Education & the Arts*. Volume 11, Number 6. Retrieved July 24, 2010 from www.ijea.org.
YouTube ABDC 4. (2009). *ABDC 4 –Vogue Evolution*. Retrieved January 8, 2011, from www.youtube.com/watch?v=bt4mI8kqzb0&feature=related.

20

CULTURAL CONVERSATIONS IN SPIRAL CURRICULUM

Olivia Gude

". . . so it was really *weird*," the student concluded. The teacher wrote on the board, describing the incident in a few words, then turned to the group and asked, "Any other weird stories?"[1] Punctuated by exclamations, incredulous looks, and cringes, the list of weird incidents grew as students recalled other personal tales of the weird (and felt increasingly comfortable sharing them). Soon after, listening to "weird music" (Steve Reich), the students made automatic scribbled drawings, delineating the moments that made up their weird stories. Later, in a hushed, darkened computer lab, the students typed furiously, capturing more aspects of the experience by uncensored automatic writing, noting every fleeting impression or association that came to mind. Then, having been scanned into Photoshop, the hand-drawn images were intertwined with the typed texts. Weird images mirroring weird stories took shape.[2]

Teacher: So, having shared our weird autobiographical images, let's figure out what is *weird*. Can we define it?
[A word web begins to form—*unusual, not normal, creepy, my neighbor, strange, off* . . .]
Teacher: But how do we decide that something is *strange* or *off*?
Student: Well, you know, you just know—it's *weird*.
Teacher: Hmm, did anyone here ever feel irritated because your parents think something is really *weird* that you think is just *normal*? How can that be?

Several students look perplexed. Others begin speaking simultaneously, struggling to put thoughts about what really constitutes *normal* or *weird* into words. One student explains, "Well, they just don't know what's going on. How you see it depends on where you are and who you know and what you've experienced before and . . . wait, wow, that's *weird*." A crack opens through which students

Cultural Conversations in Spiral Curriculum 77

It's the End of the World As We Know It, installation by teen artists and teachers of the (Dis)Order group in Spiral Workshop 2008, cut black paper and ink jet prints on wall, 35 × 11 ft.

catch a glimpse of other discursive spaces. The discussion continues. Students consider the possibility that there may be socially constructed mental walls that sharply limit their lines of sight as well as their insights, boundaries that constrain perceptions and contain thoughts.

Spiral Spaces

The space in many school classrooms is claustrophobic. The rows are straight and narrow; the places in which one is allowed to walk are clearly demarcated. There is no metaphorical room to maneuver, not enough space to move expressively. There is one right direction in which to look. Typically there is no time or place for students to look around and explore questions about things they really care about. The space of conventional curriculum is mono-dimensional. It's a world that is too flat for the kids (and teachers) to really inhabit. Vital life happens outside of school, or—if in school—in the hallways, washrooms, playgrounds, and cafeterias.

The goal of Spiral curriculum is to create spaces of inquiry, spaces for experimentation in thinking and being. Our goal is to cultivate spaces that are "out there" and "on the edge," yet are safe spaces because they are shaped and maintained by caring adults. Spiral Workshop began in 1995 as a rethinking of the Saturday teen art classes at the University of Illinois at Chicago. The curriculum is designed to be useful in community and in public-school settings.

Investigation and Participation

We think of Spiral Workshop as an ongoing collaborative art project, as an experiment in "relational aesthetics" in which youth participants are "learning to inhabit the world in a better way" (Bourriaud, 1998/2002, p. 13). In Bourriaud's formulation, much significant contemporary art is not the result of an investigation by an individual artist who reaches an endpoint or conclusion, but rather is the practice of creating frames for participatory investigation, enabling experiences that are deeply engaged and deeply reflective.

For us, the art is not just the things that students make and display, but also the lived experience and methodologies of making meaning generated through a range of individual and collaborative activities. *The Spiral Workshop Show & Community Reception* is a collective installation in which meaning is generated not solely within each student's individual art projects, but also by the interplay of meaning among the various responses to a given project, by collaborative projects, and by accompanying documentation of experiences, processes, and experiments. The unfolding, increasingly complex, and often contradictory narratives generated by sequences of projects and activities create a rich discursive space that invites viewer/participants to join the investigation. This method of display could serve as a model for re-imagining the display of school art projects in schools, creating a central role for the art teacher as a community artist convening significant community cultural discourses.

Paradoxically, though the Spiral Workshop emphasizes the collaborative construction of meaning, in today's climate in which youth (and all of us) are psychologically constrained by the designer conformity of the spectacular mass media society (as well as by real world consequences for enacting ways of being outside of the norm), collective liberatory thinking/making must begin with reconnecting to the pleasure/power potential of individual creativity, rooted in the capacity for self-absorbed reverie and release. Students (and teachers) must be able to tolerate and eventually treasure the sense of aloneness that comes from thinking/working outside of established social parameters. Being deeply invested in one's own creative experience leads to the desire to communicate, to form a community based on subtle sharing of stories, observations, and insights.

Unlike much art curriculum that is a collection of separate projects (sometimes preceded by a related technical or formal exercise), Spiral Curriculum is planned in thematic sequences. These are generative themes as described in the dialogical pedagogy of Paulo Freire (1981). These are themes that have individual and collective import, themes that will lead us into inquiries about things that matter to the participants. However, Spiral themes tend to be a bit quirky, more metaphorical than literal. We find that if we begin with a theme or big idea that is too specific *or* too abstract (such as "environmental protection" or "hope"), we can only think of art projects/activities that represent, illustrate, or symbolize what we already know and believe about the subject, rather than activities that move us—emotionally, physically, and conceptually.

Inklings

The work of making quality art curriculum has to begin the way most artworks do—with an inkling, a simultaneous knowing and not yet knowing. Then the hard work begins. Vague hunches must be embodied in specific content or vividly imagined details must be elaborated into complex curriculum structures. What if we did a group on this theme? What artists or cultural practices would we study? What kinds of things might we make? What might we find out?

A Spiral theme is a big idea intertwined with an aesthetic practice, an investigation focused by the use of particular materials or methods. Thus, these themes are essential questions, as defined in *Understanding by Design*—"key inquiries within a discipline" (Wiggins & McTighe, 2006, p. 109). Using the interdisciplinary methods of contemporary art, teachers and students engage in complex aesthetic investigations, deconstructing how meaning is made on this subject, constructing personal meaning, and reconstructing new shared cultural beliefs that form communities of understanding and care.

In 2005, a year in which "counterfeit evidence" was a major topic in understanding how the U.S. came to be at war in Iraq, the Counterfeit Evidence: Re-rendering Reality group introduced students to working in Adobe Photoshop.[3] Reconsidering family photographs and "fine art" photography, as well as images grabbed from mass media, students learned vocabulary for making and reading photographs from within classic and postmodern artistic frames and from within discourses associated with visual culture studies.

The Counterfeiters studied the problematic status of photography as evidence from its earliest days (e.g. ectoplasmic "proof" of spirits!) and contemporary controversies related to digital alteration of news photos (e.g. major British newspaper the *Evening Standard* doctoring a photograph headlined "Jubilation on the streets of Baghdad—FREEDOM" by duplicating some of the groups of people in the crowd scene to make a larger, more dramatic crowd). Student projects in this group ranged from Alternative Scrapbooking, in which students created more complex representations of family narrative than those offered in crafty culture, to a digital i-Ronic project in which students created new versions of i-Pod ads that reclaimed their human potential as self-creating I's.

Principles of Possibility

Rather than using lists of art vocabulary or media experiences as checklists for the kinds of experiences we want to include in each curriculum, we utilize a list of Principles of Possibility—*Playing, Forming Self, Investigating, Community Themes, Encountering Others, Attentive Living, Empowered Experiencing* (traditional Western and non-Western frames of aesthetics, history, and criticism as well as various visual culture approaches), *Empowered Making* (styles and methods of realism, expressionism, formalism, postmodernism, new media, and crafts), *Deconstructing Culture, Reconstructing Social Spaces,* and *Not Knowing* (Gude, 2007).[4]

The Drawing Dirty Pictures group began with students embracing mess as metaphor and as method.[5] Free-associating to see images in blots and stains, students immersed themselves in *Playing,* creating without preconceived plans. In a following *Forming Self* project, the youth artists explored personal "dirty stories," completing a worksheet that asked questions such as "Have you ever gotten in trouble for being dirty?" and "What do you try to keep clean?" It was clear that one couldn't adequately explore dirty narratives in tidy academic drawing, so the youth artists were eager to be introduced to a wide variety of artists whose work exemplified the dirty and the abject—including Francis Bacon, Camille Rose Garcia, and Mike Kelley. By the time the students began the final project *Layers of Dirt,* they were prepared for *Investigating Community Themes* and *Deconstructing Culture,* utilizing Postmodern Principles of constructing artworks such as *Appropriation, Juxtaposition, Recontextualization,* and *Layering,* to subvert the binary oppositions of clean/dirty that had previously structured their cultural imaginations and hence their personal experiences (Gude, 2004). Emblazoned above the door of the Dirty exhibition in which work was hung on smudged and fingerprinted walls was a phrase from a Hollis Sigler painting—"Mess is the stuff of life."

Reflecting on some of our theme groups over the years—including Drawing Danger: Making Monsters, Chromophobia: Painting in a Culture of Fear, Painting So Cute and Creepy, Outsider: Alternate Media, (Dis)Order, and (De)Generate—I am struck by the fact that *weird* is an appropriate descriptor for many Spiral curriculum theme choices because *weird* functions as a synonym for *not knowing*, for things that elude current conventional categories, that are irreducibly ambiguous, experiences that at least partially escape the confines of constrictive representations.

Spiral is an agency of aesthetic investigation that looks into things that are tantalizingly full of personal and cultural energy, yet whose workings in our minds lack clarity. Through projects that investigate odd and offbeat subjects (these have included punishments, bling, hauntings, reality TV, wounds, lost flyers, fluidity, warnings, uncertainty, concrete, and targets) we aim to surprise ourselves, recognizing aspects of our experiences of which we were not fully aware. Interestingly, though our subjects tend toward the shadowy side of the psyche, the projects often represent nuanced memories of deeply personal and interpersonal joyful, loving experiences that are not easily acknowledged and represented in cynical U.S. society. The goal of Spiral curriculum is not so much to definitively categorize and figure things out as to observe how the recognitions, representations, and figures of our imagination create meaning, and to then expand the discursive spaces within which these figures can move and interact, creating shifting and unforeseeable patterns of being.

Notes

1 Weird: Drawing & Computers Spiral Workshop 2009 faculty—Patrick Meers and Allison Trumbo and the 2003 Weird Drawing group led by Katherine Hoff, Jacob Mitchell, and Kara Osborne.
2 For project plans and samples of student artwork from the Weird groups and other Spiral Workshop groups mentioned in this article, see the Spiral Workshop e-Portfolio on the National Art Education: http://naea.digication.com/Spiral/Spiral_Workshop_Theme_Groups/.
3 Counterfeit Evidence: Re-rendering Reality 2005 faculty—Madi Soch and Michael Radziewicz.
4 The articles *Principles of Possibility* and *Postmodern Principles* accompanied by images of student work are posted on the Olivia Gude e-Portfolio on the National Art Education Association website: http://naea.digication.com/omg/Art_Education_Articles.
5 Drawing Dirty Pictures 2007 faculty—Alex Goldin, Christina Gowrylow, and Tazim Salik.

References

Bourriaud, N. (1998/2002). *Relational aesthetics*. (S. Pleasance & F. Woods, Trans.) Dijon, France: les presses du reel. (Original work published 1998).

Freire, P. (1981). *Pedagogy of the oppressed*. New York: The Continuum Publishing Corporation. (Original work published in 1970.)

Gude, O. (2004). Postmodern principles: In search of a 21st century art education. *Art Education, 53*(1), 6–14.

Gude, O. (2007). Principles of possibility: Considerations for a 21st century art and culture curriculum. *Art Education, 60*(1), 6–17.

Wiggins, G., & McTighe, J. (2006). *Understanding by design* (2nd ed.). Upper Saddle River, NJ: Pearson Education.

21
ARTS MAKING AS AN ACT OF THEORY

Miia Collanus and Tiina Heinonen

Introduction

We are a teacher (Miia Collanus) and a student (Tiina Heinonen) from a study program for future textile teachers at the University of Helsinki, Finland. Having studied and worked in the textile teacher study program, Miia felt that teacher students are not encouraged to critically think about the cultural position of the craft teacher or the subject craft. Dominated by cognitive psychology, the focus of their education is on the learning situations and craft processes without exploring the cultural and social contexts of craft and education. The underlying problem is that knowledge is taken as something pre-determined. Hence, students are taught that a textile teacher has the role of a mediator instead of encouraging them to explore a particular subject position of the textile teacher as a producer and reproducer of culture and society. Crucially, in this concept of knowledge, the making of crafts, which is the primary activity of textile lessons, is left outside the realm of theory. No wonder implementing social and cultural aspects may seem a difficult task after graduation.

If theory is understood as a set of material and contextual practices instead of a ready-made cognitive tool that embellishes arts lessons, a range of new possibilities for critical arts pedagogy and social justice education opens up; teaching becomes a contextual activity that shifts the focus of learning from creative self-expression to self-awareness, from artifact and skilled knowledge to cultural context and action. Viewing arts making as an act of theory moves the focus away from describing the content to understanding the context. As an example, instead of focusing on skills and design, knitting could be used as a medium for exploring such issues as feminism and femininity. For example, while preparing an installation for a public place that represents masculinity, pupils develop self-awareness and learn that they are in a position to transform culture.

84 Miia Collanus and Tiina Heinonen

Tiina Heinonen and Saara Kumpulainen, *Textile Crafts for Girls, Woodwork for Boys?*, 2010, picture collage

In this article, Miia describes how cultural studies theories offer a ground for critical arts pedagogy where the arts making is a key medium for grasping the cultural and social. To illustrate, she presents an assignment from her teaching where students materialized a research methodology. In closing, Tiina presents her materialization of gendered craft education.

Textile Craft Education in Finland

In Finnish elementary school, craft is a compulsory subject located in the category of "arts" along with visual art, music and physical education. The foundations of textile craft education lie in design studies and cognitive psychology, and the objective is on the design and making processes of textile products. The techniques most used are knitting, crocheting, sewing, embroidery, and felting.

Although officially gender neutral, how the teaching is organized reproduces gender divisions. To begin with, craft is actually a *combined* subject area constructed out of textile crafts and technical crafts (wood, metal, electronics). In most schools, from the fifth grade onward pupils have to choose which crafts to concentrate on. Almost all boys choose technical crafts and most girls textile crafts. For a ten or eleven year old, this stereotypical choice is difficult to resist, because all textile teachers are women and most technical teachers are male. The teacher education for each, too, is organized into two different study programs in different universities and in two distinct disciplinary locations.

Arts Making as an Act of Theory

The dominant view of theory is that it is stable and fixed, or as in postmodern art education, that it is a set of representations of reality. In this essentialist view, theory remains in the background of arts lessons and thus is challenging to implement in arts teaching since it does not belong to the realm of making. But, if we take seriously the idea of theory as a process, we are in a position to rearticulate the theory–practice dichotomy.

First we need to understand the contingency of culture, that instead of a thing, culture is *a process* constructed within various social practices in particular historical contexts. Thus, theory, too, is a context-dependent process constantly changing in social practices. Theory and practice are actually inseparable, or even, there is nothing but practice and theory is like an arbitrary closure, something to begin with. Hence, arts making is actually a process of theorizing. To transform this idea of theory into arts pedagogy means shifting the focus from the content to the contexts of making. However, the contexts of making are not just as a background to reflect on or situations surrounding the making, but relational cultural structures that are available for rearticulation in the making of arts. Our position as teachers is to make the relatedness of the contexts explicit and encourage pupils to produce better descriptions of culture. (Grossberg, 2006; Hall, 1997; Slack, 1996.)

For example, instead of introducing the Finnish tradition of embroidery as techniques and products, we could ask pupils to explore who embroiderers are (and are not), where embroidery is practiced and what products are made. When they realize that most embroiderers are women in domestic settings making functional products, we could ask them to think and discuss, while embroidering, how they identify themselves in this context and what kind of a culture of embroidery they want to produce. By making a collective embroidered project for members of the parliament demanding more democratic societies, pupils can have the experience of using making to create new ideas.

The Materializing Methodology

When I began to develop this kind of a contextual pedagogy for crafts teaching, I was teaching a course on cultural studies methodologies for home economics and textile craft teacher students. It consisted of my lectures, articles, and an essay assignment. When I realized how difficult the idea of contingency in cultural studies was for the students who had been socialized into the idea of knowledge being something predetermined, I began to wonder whether methodological knowledge could be demonstrated with another mode of thinking than writing. To replace the essay, I created an assignment titled "critical gaze" where I asked the students to choose one problematic area from their fields of study to materialize in a mode other than written text using cultural studies theories and methods. They were allowed to choose materials and techniques themselves. I encouraged them to work in groups to promote a dialogue among different perspectives.

The materializations varied from collages of pictures cut from magazines and glued on cardboard to three-dimensional installations. A group of home economics students constructed a place setting representing the idea of good food in home economics as an articulation of discourses of diet and homemade food. Another group explored the identity of the home economics teacher as an articulation of national domesticity and innovative multiculturalism. Their collage consisted of two female figures that were connected by the idea of skilled making, which represented the mode of the connection.

I was surprised by how inspiring the students found the assignment and how the cultural studies theories and the idea of contingency became easier for them. It is my hope that they also learned that theorizing is not a matter of a medium, but that any medium can function as a tool with which to grasp the context. I believe that this kind of assignment could be used more extensively in university teaching to enrich the dominance of linguistics.

Tiina: A Critical Gaze on Gender in Textile Craft Education

I did my critical gaze assignment with Saara Kumpulainen, who also studies in the textile teacher study program. We chose to focus on the gender division in textile crafts because although this issue is deeply embedded in the context of textile crafts, in our studies this topic was less analyzed. We wanted to question the taken-for-granted conceptions of gender in craft and to encourage the viewers to critically look for stereotypical masculinities and femininities in the culture of craft. We used the cultural studies idea of articulation and re-articulation and constructed the unusual articulations of the hegemonic discourses of craft and gender. We chose excerpts from newspapers, research reports, and Internet message boards that described gender and craft and constructed figures that performed the hegemonic discourses in unexpected ways. Using text excerpts and figures together created re-articulations combining "reality" and "fiction" and enabled the questioning of what is "normal."

The picture collage on page 84 is one example of these re-articulations in our course work. In this example, we wanted to explore how the discourses of femininity and masculinity are naturalized in the context of craft. For example, dexterity is seen as feminine, while masculinity is constructed on the premises of rationality and agency. In a quote from a newspaper, a female textile teacher says: "There are differences between boys and girls in terms of dexterity. For example, the boys are used to technical work and therefore handle pins as if they were nails" (Palokari, 2006). To challenge this stereotype of dexterity as a female ability and as related particularly to textile crafts, we placed alongside the textile teacher's quote the Finnish entertainer Danny, who constructs his public image on the premises of hegemonic masculinity. We dressed Danny in a black suit and showed him making lace with graceful hands, representing an articulation of two opposite discourses: the conservatively dressed, masculine male and a craft technique that symbolizes femininity and dexterity. We wanted to ask why the text excerpt seems "real" and the figure absurd.

In preparing the critical gaze, we materialized not only the methodology, but also a concrete problematic in the school context. For me, disconnecting methodology from its traditional location was not only an interesting way to study methodology, but it also gave me pedagogical tools with which to explore the cultural and social in craft making—with the media typical of craft. Constructing articulations and re-articulations of gender also made me think about how cultural discourses effect in classroom and my practices as a textile craft teacher.

Theorizing for Social Justice

In the end, the question of the theory–practice dichotomy is about the politics of knowledge. What is considered as valid knowledge in current neoliberal policies becomes ever more important. As arts educators, we must struggle to gain more status for our subjects by highlighting in all instances that theory is not only a cognitive act, but also a sensuous and practical activity (cf. Kincheloe, 2004, 2008).

Viewing arts making as an act of theory entails taking theory as a proposal, an invitation for grasping the context with the media of arts. This view moves the focus from the content to the context placing the process of making instead of the artifact as the objective of arts education. The process of exploring the contexts to find cultural articulations, then deconstructing them into pieces and finally re-articulating the found elements in new and surprising ways is a powerful tool for imagining utopian futures and challenging hegemonic discourses. Pupils learn *while* making that culture is a result of various decisions that could always have been made differently. They become aware that what is known as "our culture" is not a homogeneous entity, but consists of various competing ideologies. They also learn that art and craft are not atheoretical and that through making artifacts we produce culture. As critical arts pedagogues, it is our responsibility to guide pupils to these moments of awareness, to give them voice and agency.

References

Grossberg, L. (2006). Does cultural studies have futures? Should it? (Or what's the matter with New York?) *Cultural Studies, 20*(1), 1–32.

Hall, S. (1997). Introduction. In S. Hall (Ed.), *Representation: Cultural representations and signifying practices* (pp. 1–12). London: Sage.

Kincheloe, J. L. (2004). *Critical pedagogy primer.* New York: Peter Lang Publishing.

Kincheloe, J. L. (2008). *Knowledge and critical pedagogy: An introduction.* Dordrecht, Netherlands: Springer.

Palokari, Sirpa. 2006. Poikienkin laji. *Lapsen maailma 9*, 40–42. (Helsinki: Central Union for Child Welfare).

Slack, D. J. (1996). The theory and method of articulation. In K-H. Chen & D. Morley (Eds.), *Stuart Hall: Critical dialogues in cultural studies* (pp. 112–127). London: Routledge.

22

PEDAGOGY, COLLABORATION, AND TRANSFORMATION

A Conversation with Brett Cook

Korina Jocson and Brett Cook

Brett Cook is an artist–educator who seeks to innovate teaching and learning beyond the classroom. For over two decades, Brett has produced a range of projects, including paintings, drawings, photographs, and installations, in various parts of the U.S. and around the world. A product of public educators, he has worked side-by-side with other artists and students across educational settings. I was introduced to Brett's artwork in 2000 during a public exhibition of paintings about the history and culture of Barbados. I was there studying education in Caribbean societies. It was clear to me then that Brett's work exemplifies—both symbolically and artistically—the *collaboration and transformation* that invite youth and adults alike to contemplate the pedagogical possibilities in education. To me as an educator, both collaboration and transformation affirm the importance of centering on the funds of knowledge of local actors and expand the nature of learning as a dynamic co-constructed experience.

In May of 2010, Brett and I had an opportunity to talk about art and education. He was in the middle of preparing for a solo exhibit called *Supernatural* in San Francisco. While discussing current and future works, he revealed a well-anticipated collaboration with The Living Word Project sponsored by Youth Speaks, a literary arts organization based in San Francisco serving youth ages 13–19. I was intrigued, given my interest in literacy and youth cultural studies. In our conversation, collaboration and transformation resurfaced and are worth highlighting here as part of the book's themes.

KORINA JOCSON (KJ): Art has been a big part of your life. You have produced and shared so much with so many different people. How did you get started? And what does it mean to you?
BRETT COOK (BC): Creativity has been a source of joy for me my entire life. Since early childhood when my mother gave me slips of paper to draw on

Brett Cook, *Coloring Pauli Murray at The Pauli Murray Birthday Celebration*, November 2007, paint pen and oil pastel on non-woven media, 16 × 12 ft.

Brett Cook, *Recognizing Different Worlds: Art, Social Change, and Documentary*, Spring 2008, variable dimensions. Faculty, students, staff, and community residents presented their work for the day. The class separated into five groups with Polaroid cameras and created a visual alphabet, considering concept and technique in the object of their creation as well as its presentation to the entire group. Shown also are artifacts in process from previous social collaborations and community generated rubrics.

to keep me occupied, the creation of images and stories and space within myself has been a celebration. My early products hung on classroom walls and family refrigerators as suggestions of their value to others, but I first and foremost connected to something wonderful about the process of making things for myself.

As I made more things, I became more skillful in crafting products and my concept of creativity shifted to more deeply considering that final product. From my first day of Kindergarten through my Bachelors of Fine Arts college degree, I learned that being a great artist—like a choreographer, musician, or a painter—meant that I should make great things. I've now come to understand that part of being a skillful artist transcends any discipline. Being a great artist is best manifested in how I create my life. I've been inspired by venture capitalists, chefs, and teachers who were incredible artists in the way they thought about logarithms, the chemistry of flavors, peer-generated curriculum, and the way they lived their authentic everyday lives. Conversely, I've learned from artists who danced on stages, performed concerts, or shown at New York galleries who suffer through a way living that doesn't reflect their true self.

In my art and life, I aspire to be open to the spectrum of experiences that reflect my unique self. On the one hand, I have a more conventional, Western artistic practice where I come to a studio and make things by myself; and then on the other, I will sometimes work with groups of people, and I may not make any objects. I may co-develop curriculum or methodologies, but the things are made by the other participants—and "things" include objects, ideas, and new ways of being. I also have countless ratios between these extremes of solitary artist and community catalyst. I don't think of a hierarchy in the variety of my artistic practice where one extreme of participation is better than another or one is more valuable. I aspire to see my art as a diverse reflection of my aspirations, aesthetics, and existence in the ongoing creation of my life.

KJ: Could you elaborate on this spectrum and how it ties to your teaching practice?

BC: A central part of my teaching practice is concerned with skillfully building healthy environments where participants can document *transformation* and magnify awareness. I believe that there are opportunities for personal transformation and magnified awareness in all subjects, all cultures, all things. Regardless of what I am teaching, I aspire to find access to different disciplines and infinite mechanisms to cultivate people's awareness and create reflection and action. I aspire to cultivate a problem posing experience in dialogue across disciplines that can benefit everyone.

KJ: If you were to envision art and education, what kinds of things would you like to see pedagogically? What would those things entail?

BC: I think I would not label it as "art and education." I would just call it education. And I know sometimes people are challenged by such a general title because they want art to be recognized. Sometimes it feels important to have the "art" with education because it can feel like art making is absent without that acknowledgment. But in my belief of education, art is one vehicle of a larger process of personal evolution, transformation, and enlightenment. I think that for me it's an essential vehicle, which is different from the way traditional, conventional, American education is typically taught today. Legislation and funding cuts frequently subtract art from schools, a tangible sign that art is not thought of as essential. My belief is that art is not greater than or less than other disciplines. As an educator, I want people to nurture their whole selves. As a teacher and as a learner, I try to cultivate our complex nature and make us all more humane, which is beyond any singular subject. Because of the structure and the expectation of institutions, there is typically little space to cultivate multidisciplinary administrators, teachers, or students.

KJ: So, in a way, it is rethinking education.

BC: I see education as a process for transformation. Education is more than importing facts to memory, more than banking education or a theoretical understanding of problem-posing pedagogy. Education is a practice of cultivating a mind without limits, transcending bad habits, and recognizing wisdom through countless vehicles for learning.

KJ: Many have described your work as collaborative. How do you define collaborative? How do you and participants create collaborative projects? What's the process like? Would you say that there is a redistribution of power?

BC: When I was younger, I used to think *collaboration* meant that I have an idea, you can help me do it, and we'll call it collaboration. At this point, I think of collaboration as a practice that participants, including myself, contribute to in reciprocal ways in both the conceptual process and product. Because we all have expertise that we share in the manifestation of that collective action. So oftentimes in groups I'll teach collaboration as breathing together. I'll have an exercise where I will say, "Let's take three breaths together." To me, that's a collaboration. That's something we all had to do, we all wanted to do it, and we each did it in our own ways. Some people take longer inhales, some people use more of their diaphragm, some people puff out their stomach but it's something that we all did together. And so I think of collaboration in that kind of framework. When I'm in a classroom or when I'm on a project, part of the work is finding out what are the things that we all want to do. It starts with asking what do we as participants think is important. What do we all as collaborators define individually and collectively as authentic?

KJ: What do you mean?

BC: Like what is something valuable here, where we are right now, who is here that we can each offer and name together? And then how do we nurture the different expertise in our group to experience and enhance our collective values? For example, I know a good deal about drawing. I like to draw, and I'm pretty good at it. If there's a part of the collaboration that requires drawing, that would be a good part of the work for me to do. In collaboration we constantly discover the pieces that we each have expertise and then combine them to work together. In the ongoing discovery process that is collaboration, dialogue, deep listening, and learning have to constantly occur. The results of that process can result in engaging objects, evolved ideas, and new ways of being.

KJ: In other words, it's about a sharing of that time and space, the doing.

BC: Well, that's kind of why I describe it as creating an environment where people can learn. I try to build the environment and some of that is physical, some of that is intellectual, some of that is emotional and some of that is spiritual where learning can occur. And part of building a fertile learning environment is simply modeling, or being acutely responsible for my actions. That might mean we're simply going to speak to each other using first names out of respect and equality. It might mean repeatedly making time to assess our expectations, so that it becomes apparent we have a shared agenda. The learning environment is a synthesis of many actions, to cultivate relationships where people learn to teach themselves, and to create spaces where people feel inspired to look at themselves and transform.

KJ: So, how might this look like in a classroom? What might one say initially to draw out expertise, to create an environment where there is that kind of sharing?

BC: Well, for me, it takes some unlearning of habits to create space for our true nature to manifest. So we can get outside of expectations that have been cultivated by our educational history and personal histories that prevent us from being open. Interestingly, when I was younger, I used to think that my art and education was about helping other people to be better and giving them all this data that then would help them be empowered and transform the world. And now I realize education hinges on my own transformation. How can I be the person that listens deeply to everyone? How can I be more flexible and invested in what other people are interested in? How can I present in class the best work that I can in the same assignments that I expect of my students? How can I be that patient, enthusiastic, mindful, generous and disciplined practitioner? How can I be my best model of this idea of collaboration, and be compassionate when other people can't do it?

KJ: It is a model of transformation at the personal and professional level.

BC: To transform myself, that certainly can be affected by the environment but ultimately it's in my own mind. As an educator it poses the question of how I take responsibility for my own transformation, as a teacher. If I'm really committed to transforming the world, let me transform myself and then by the nature of that ongoing evolution with awareness everything in my world will change. To affect the future, heal the past, or transform the relationship to others is to be concerned with my own transformation in the present moment, and change the way that I live in the world. Who I am is reflected in everything that I do—my interpersonal relationships, my professional relationship, where I shop, what I eat. When the anger, mistrust, or fear that keeps me separate from others is transformed, that is radical social change.

KJ: A process of interconnectedness.

BC: Yes, which is part of why I think collaboration is an essential and a powerful mechanism for learning. It exemplifies interconnectedness in very tangible ways.

Samples of Brett Cook's work

From *Face Up: Telling Stories of Community Life*, collaborative project in Durham, North Carolina

Face Up engaged more than 1,500 people in a series of events to foster new connections and dialogue and to expand awareness of local history. The project was anchored in a semester-long class "Recognizing Different Worlds: Art, Social Change, and Documentary." The campus–community collaboration project together with the Recognizing Different Worlds class culminated with 14 permanent public artworks across six neighborhoods, and a large-scale exhibition at the Center for Documentary Studies at Duke University. Now installed on the exterior walls of businesses, schools, and other publicly accessible places across Durham, the artworks document the creative involvement of toddlers, school-aged children, high-school and college students, professors, and elders; the wealthy and the working class; and African American, Latino, Anglo, and Asian neighborhood residents. The project opened artistic and documentary processes to many groups and individuals whose paths had never crossed. For more information, visit www.brett-cook.com.

PART III
Toward Futures
Social and Personal Transformation

INTRODUCTION

The Next Big Thing

Lisa Hochtritt

>What was that bang? It was the next big thing
>Exploding over our heads
>And soon the next generation
>Will emerge from behind the bike sheds
>What are we going to offer them?
>The exact same thing as before
>But a different way to wear it
>And the promise of a whole lot more
>
>   Billy Bragg, 1985

Young people possess the power to create their own cultures and develop their own futures, now like never before. Contributors in this section address changing educational landscapes where students and artists are uploading and sharing content, not just downloading it. There is a promise of more participation, collaboration, and communication in sustained and varying ways, moving beyond the tradition school walls and allowing students to be critical producers of their own cultures, not just consumers. Schubert (2010) explains how public pedagogy and chances to learn beyond formal schooling are critical:

>Focus on curriculum and pedagogy in schooling alone represents a myopic view of what shapes human beings. . . . It is crucial that individuals and grassroots communities see education as a search for who and how they are becoming—to see themselves as developers of curricula, *currere*, and public pedagogies as they more fully find who they are and hope to be.
>
>   *(2010, p. 16)*

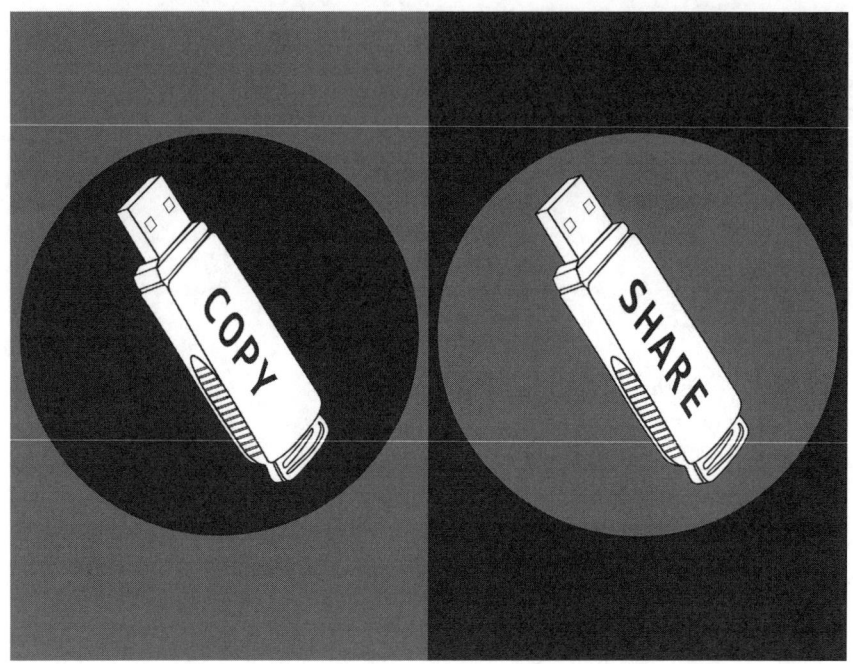

Designated Drivers, 2011. Twenty artists and groups each put up to 4 GB of their archives, research, films, videos, software, images, etc. on USB drives. You are invited to copy everything! Organized by Temporary Services. www.temporaryservices.org

The authors in Part III offer up possibilities of what's next. Traditional schooling alone cannot provide for our futures, and the artists, educators, and cultural workers in this section discuss new pedagogies for social and personal transformation.

Exploding Over Our Heads

Social networks are omnipresent. Smartphones, Facebook, Twitter, and YouTube fill up our time and connect us, urging our attention be spent in fractured tidbits. Juan Carlos Castro writes about Harrell Fletcher's work, suggesting new ideas about social interactions and connecting media. He argues that social practice is new media. Jorge Lucero's considers an alternative blurring of the public and private and how La Pocha Nostra grapples with transparent lines in their performance work. And Steven Ciampaglia discusses Pinky & Bunny, an artist's group that produces free, cat-image-driven, educational animations available on the Internet.

The Exact Thing as Before, But a Different Way to Wear It

There is lasting power in documenting everyday culture and that which already exists. Lisa Yun Lee explores how the Chiapas Photography Project's documentary photographs are activist acts and how recording the traditional is a common act of self-determination. Maritza Bautista writes about Appalshop's long-standing dialogue, activism, and organizing that have contributed to discourse on traditions of documenting stories from one's community. And Sharif Bey reflects on the importance of connecting personal narratives and shared experiences of the past to understanding one's own biases and fears.

Creating art and education in unexpected places is something these next authors have in common. As the collective group Temporary Services states, "Experiencing art in the places we inhabit on a daily basis remains a critical concern for us. It helps us move art from a privileged experience to one more directly related to how we live our lives." Artist Navjot Altaf does just this; as explored in Manisha Sharma's essay, Altaf helps her public participants question who is the *public* in public art? Educators Carol Culp and Rubén Gaztambide-Fernández also challenge expectations, discussing collaboratively how and where learning happens.

And the Promise of a Whole Lot More

Embracing Greene's idea of "imagining things as if they could be otherwise" (1988, p. 3), authors A. Laurie Palmer, B. Stephen Carpenter, II and Marissa Muñoz, and Raimundo Martins take on issues of social and environmental justice. They consider how artists and educators can contribute to the conversation on equalizing power through art, ideas, public education, and action. As the contributors in this section confirm, the arts, collective practices and public pedagogies hold great promise in thinking toward our futures and re-envisioning how participation in education can happen in more democratic and transformational ways.

References

Bragg, B. (1985). I don't need this pressure Ron. On *Days like these* (7 inch). UK: Go Discs. Lyrics retrieved on March 18, 2011 from www.lyricsfreak.com/b/billy+bragg/i+dont+need+this+pressure+ron_20018246.html

Greene, M. (1988). *The dialectic of freedom*. New York: Teachers College Press.

Schubert, W. H. (2010). Outside curricula and public pedagogy. In J. Sandlin, B. Schultz, & J. Burdick (Eds.), *Handbook of public pedagogy: Education and learning beyond schooling* (pp. 10–17). New York: Routledge.

Temporary Services. (n.d.). Contact. Retrieved on March 18, 2011 from www.temporaryservices.org/contact.html

23

HARRELL FLETCHER

Shaping a New Social

Juan Carlos Castro

> I am getting along nicely in the dark.
> *(An excerpt from James Joyce's Ulysses (Joyce, 1960) read by Walter Cutler in Harrell Fletcher's The Problem of Possible Redemption, 2003)*

In Harrell Fletcher's collaborative video, *The Problem of Possible Redemption*, seniors from the Parkville Senior Center in Connecticut read lines from James Joyce's novel *Ulysses*. The video consists of a series of close-up shots, through a wide-angle lens, of seniors reading from cue cards, pausing to address the camera periodically. The technical crafting of the video is honest and intimate in its simplicity and proximity to the seniors. *Ulysses*'s themes of "society, war, and personal morality" told by seniors at a close distance puts the viewer in a position rarely experienced. *The Problem of Possible Redemption* (see Plate 17) can be initially interpreted as a video document of seniors reading excerpts from a novel, but upon further analysis it can also be construed as an occasion to consider the voice of seniors and their collective wisdom, as told through the stream-of-consciousness work of *Ulysses*.

This artwork and many others by Harrell Fletcher exemplify his artistic inquiry through social practice. The traditional tools and media that we associate with art making—drawing, painting, sculpture, photography, and video—are present in many of his art works, yet the *work of art* is the practice of shaping new kinds of social encounters. In *The Problem of Possible Redemption*, we encounter people from an important and growing part of our communities in a different way. What Fletcher and his art do is ask participants, viewers, and makers to reconsider their habitual interpretations and engagements with others. Though it is not a guarantee for a more socially just encounter, understandings prompted from such experiences provide an occasion to think and act differently about one's complicity in the social structures we create and perpetuate.

Harrell Fletcher, *The Problem of Possible Redemption*, 2003, a video adaptation of James Joyce's *Ulysses* shot at the Parkville Senior Center, Connecticut (running time 13 minutes 25 seconds)

The Problem of Possible Redemption points to possibilities for art education that rethink traditional media and processes taught in art classrooms. It does not replace traditional teaching of media, rather it suggests how the social—the habitual and patterned contexts, relations, interactions, and perceptions between people—is a *medium* in itself. How can we reshape local contexts, communities, and social practices, even if for a moment, to bring us new understandings of each other? This is a question that underlies much of the public and community art in North America and relational aesthetics of European art practice of the last 20 years. Fletcher reflects,

> Since I've been paying attention, it's become incredibly obvious how few meaningful questions people ask each other. I recommend that people try a little harder. How much do you really know about the people who you encounter on a daily basis?
>
> *(Fletcher, 2002, p. 5)*

If we think of the medium of an artwork as an opportunity for shaping new social encounters, we can then consider how works of art can meaningfully create opportunities for social and personal transformation.

References

Fletcher, H. (2002). Towards a tender society of thoughtful questions and answers. Retrieved August 25, 2010, from www.harrellfletcher.com/index3b.html

Joyce, J. (1960). *Ulysses*. London: Bodley Head.

24

PINKY & BUNNY

Critical Pedagogy 2.0

Steven Ciampaglia

The future of activist art and media is going to the cats. Well, at least one cat in particular: Pinky, the star of *The Pinky Show*, an animated series featured on YouTube, devoted to informing viewers about controversial political issues often ignored by mainstream commercial media.

Most episodes of *The Pinky Show* (see Plate 18) take the form of a mock news broadcast that commences with Pinky, an animated black and white tabby, sitting behind an anchor desk. In a demure, childlike voice that is the epitome of sweetness, Pinky introduces the topic for the episode and proceeds to explore that topic with a probing yet gentle curiosity. There's no mistaking Pinky's gentle tone for naïveté, for her exploration of topics is thorough and provocative. For instance, in an episode entitled *Re: Structure, Power & Agency*, Pinky ponders "how the First World can keep turning a blind eye toward what we created" and muses that "the way we have chosen to live is the thing that binds us to all those hungry children and drowning polar bears." In another episode, *The Health Care Crisis, Part 1*, Pinky interviews medical physician and economist, Dr. Hui, who explains that "skyrocketing healthcare costs" are "a leading cause of bankruptcies," both business and personal, contributing to the volatility of the world economy.

While topics like these are weighty, the adorable, Hello Kitty-like stylization of the animation employed by *The Pinky Show*'s creators, known publicly only as Pinky & Bunny, makes these heady topics more accessible to young adult viewers. The availability of *The Pinky Show* via YouTube also increases the likelihood that these topics will reach their intended audience of young people, who comprise a huge portion of YouTube's user base (Jenkins, 2006).

Distributing *The Pinky Show* via YouTube also allows viewers to participate in creating an online culture dedicated to the program. YouTube's Comments

Pinky & Bunny (*The Pinky Show*), *Pinky Visits the Principal's Office*. Pinky Show comic number 5, 2011, 20½ × 15 in.

feature provides viewers with a forum to discuss the socio-political subject matter presented in each animation by posting their views upon the particular topic addressed in that episode. Devotees can subscribe to *The Pinky Show*'s YouTube channel and be alerted whenever a new installment of the program is posted. They can also use YouTube's Share function, and with a single click, disseminate *The Pinky Show* animations to a myriad of users of social media networks like Facebook, MySpace, Twitter, etc. Fans can also embed episodes within their own personal blogs, and alert subscribers to their blogs whenever they do so.

By using online art projects such as *The Pinky Show* as a model, art educators can create projects that will bring critical pedagogical discourse within the field into the twenty-first century. This will ensure that socially conscientious art instruction can continue to reach its desired audience of young people and affect in them a transformation of consciousness that can contribute to positive social change in a culture increasingly mediated by new communication technologies.

References

Jenkins, H. (2006). *Convergence culture: Where old and new media collide.* New York: New York University Press.

25

LA POCHA NOSTRA

Practicing Mere Life

Jorge Lucero

Artists are often taught that as makers of culture and ideas they can look to the formulations and concepts of other artists in order to further their own practices. Whether it's called appropriation, inspiration, creative response, or flat-out stealing, artists—regardless of their age, expertise, academic level, or even interest in contemporary art—make use of the manifold pluralities in current art discourses to participate in those very conversations that they borrow from. The use of contemporary art in art education continues to have a somewhat modernist lean toward productivity even if the artwork that is being used doesn't readily qualify as a typical modernist object.

Some artists' processes—particularly polyglots who work through multiple mediums and strategies—propose that we shift our pedagogical foci away from the production of art objects and language to an artist's mode of operation and possibly even to an artist's mere life practices. For example, La Pocha Nostra (LPN) (see Plate 19) is a San Francisco artists' collective that is usually categorized as performance-based. Guillermo Gómez-Peña—one of the founders of the group— described co-founder Roberto Sifuentes and himself as, "first and foremost conceptual artists" (Gómez-Peña et al., 2000, p. 171), explaining later in the interview that "half of the work [we] do is in the civic realm rather than in the art world, but it goes unnoticed . . . the art world is simply not interested in these other activities" (p. 185). Gómez-Peña points out that these acts of direct activism —such as affiliating themselves with the Farm Labor Organizing Committee— are perceived by the art world as "parallel activities" (p. 185) to LPN's "real" work. These "parallel activities" magnify an aspect of LPN's practice that is difficult to codify for curriculum development because "mere life" is situational, personal, palimpsestic, and often inarticulatable. Sifuentes's website biography describes him not as an interdisciplinary performance artist but simply as an "interdisciplinary

La Pocha Nostra: Guillermo Gómez-Peña, Roberto Sifuentes, and Violeta Luna

performance" (La Pocha Nostra, 2010, p. 1); that is, Sifuentes's entire existence falls under this moniker and as such is impossible to replicate either in its form, content, or pedagogy.

Performances where the "otherness" of LPN's participants is accented via theatrics in order to perform "the multiplicity of mythologies and perceptions of Mexicans and Chicanos in the US" (Sifuentes as quoted in Gómez-Peña et al., 2000, p. 170) is one of the group's public gestures, which could be seen as curriculizable. However, in tandem with LPN's less seen "parallel" works of social activism these theatrical works become more nuanced, encouraging creative respondents not just to watch, mimic, or analyze LPN, but to *practice* La Pocha Nostra. The observer is invited to blur the public activists' pedagogical and creative dealings, which have more visibility with the private everyday acts of conversation, caring, studying, and planning that usually remain latent in creative social engagement. Presented as an alternative to the aesthetic curriculizing of LPN's work, practicing LPN through this purposeful blurring of the public and the private offers creative practitioners the opportunity to create their own powerful *mesclas* (mixtures).

References

Gómez-Peña, G., Sifuentes, R., & Wolford, L. (2000). Away from the surveillance cameras of the art world: Strategies for collaboration and community activism. In G. Gómez-Peña (Ed.), *Dangerous border crossers: The artist talks back* (pp. 167–187). London: Routledge.

La Pocha Nostra (2010). *Who are Pocha? Roberto Sifuentes*. Retrieved June 3, 2010 from www.pochanostra.com/who/

26
FUTURE FARMERS
Leaping Over the Impossible Present

A. Laurie Palmer

Future Farmers is an artist collective and design studio whose projects actively engage participants and viewers in re-imagining the intersections of human and natural systems from a perspective of social and environmental justice and public education. Their inspiring, critical, playful, and visionary projects not only propose concrete changes to existing systems, but also expose the susceptibility of these systems to change, inviting us to engage with and continue this important work.

Artist Amy Franceschini founded Future Farmers in 1995, and the group now includes Dan Allende, Sasha Merg, Josh On, Stijn Schiffeleers, and Michael Swaine, as well as an ever-changing network of collaborators who come together for a particular project. Participants' diverse skills and interests provide a strong foundation for a practice that spans installation, sculpture, performance, design, new media, public art, and public education. The collective articulates its focus broadly as "a group of practitioners aligned through an open practice of making work that is relevant to the time and space surrounding us" (www.futurefarmers. org). Specific projects have proposed radical re-inventions of food, water, waste, and energy systems. Future Farmers often work with scientists but the technical aspect of their work remains accessible, in line with their focus on public education. Their work often develops over time through residencies that allow them to connect a community of people with the resources of an institution, embodying the spirit of a radical free school.

Sometimes the group puts decision-making directly into the hands of a systems-user. The three drains of *Rainwater Harvester/Greywater System Feedback Loop* "allow ... you to decide to let your water run back into ... storage units, into the greywater system to the garden, or out to the city system" (where it would be wasted) (www.futurefarmers.com/). Future Farmers' 2007 *Victory*

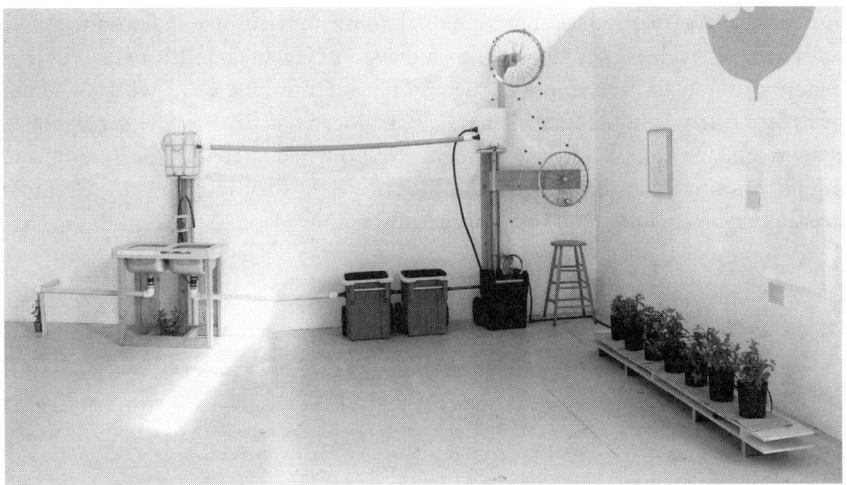

Amy Franceschini and Michael Swaine, *Rainwater Harvester/Greywater System Feedback Loop*, 2007, wood, steel, plastic, mint, rubber, 18 × 12 × 3 ft.

Gardens project (see Plates 20a and 20b) in San Francisco remembers and revives the massive urban gardening program that was implemented during the Second World War to address wartime food shortages. In the contemporary context, when the post-Second World War industrial agriculture expansion has proven to be both toxic and unsustainable, and during a time of endless war, this civic-scale undertaking brilliantly revives a choice we made but didn't pursue, and offers a second chance to gain more direct control over our food, land, and growing systems.

The work of Future Farmers bridges past and future, leaping over the impossible present—a present in which healthcare, education, and housing are de-prioritized, bankers get bonuses while unemployment skyrockets, and our food is largely made of fossil fuels. The projects of Future Farmers gain traction and duration, and garner significant attention, because they are able to light the public imagination, even as they function on a grassroots level. The inclusive and social nature of the collective amplifies the efficacy and meaning of its work, whether participants are artists, designers, engineers, politicians, activists, writers, neighbors, singers, and/or farmers. Future Farmers give body, concreteness, possibility, and momentum to what some might call utopian ideas; they invite us to help build this bridge and also to walk on it to get to another place.

12 Kimsooja, *Mumbai: A Laundry Field*, 2007, C-Print, 35 × 28⅝ in.

13 Xu Bing, *Book from the Sky*, 1987–1991, hand printed books, ceiling and wall scrolls printed from wood letterpress type using false Chinese characters, dimensions variable. Installation view at *Crossings*, National Gallery of Canada, Ottawa, 1998, dimensions variable

14 Bernard Williams, *Charting America*, installation view at State of Illinois Museum, Chicago, 2010, painted wood and found objects, dimensions variable

15 Hock E Aye Vi Edgar Heap of Birds, *Beyond the Chief*, a 12-panel public art installation of signage (defaced) at the University of Illinois, Urbana campus

16 Samuel Fosso, *La femme libérée américaine dans des années 70*, 1997

17 Harrell Fletcher, *The Problem of Possible Redemption*, 2003, a video adaptation of James Joyce's *Ulysses* shot at the Parkville Senior Center, Connecticut (running time 13 minutes 25 seconds)

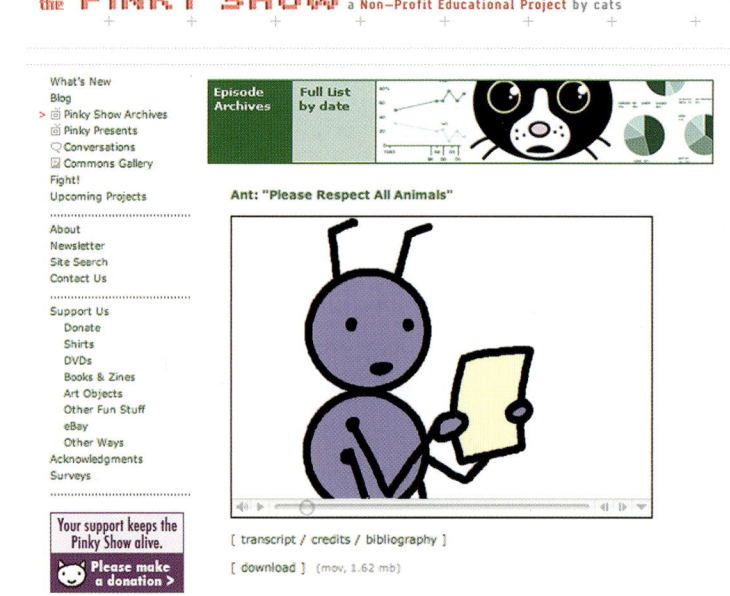

18 Pinky & Bunny (*The Pinky Show*), *Ant Appeal: "Please Respect All Animals,"* 2006, video (running time 2 minutes 27 seconds)

19 La Pocha Nostra: Guillermo Gómez-Peña, Roberto Sifuentes, Violeta Luna

20a Victory Gardens Located Across From City Hall, 1943, San Francisco

20b Amy Franceschini/Future Farmers, *Victory Gardens*, 2007, San Francisco, dimensions variable

21 Elizabeth Barret, *Stranger with a Camera*, 2000, Hugh O'Connor, Elizabeth Barret, Hobart Ison (left to right), 16 mm color film finished on video (running time 61 minutes)

22 Navjot Altaf, *Delhi Loves Me?*, 2005. Stickers installed on 15,000 autorickshaws in Khirki and Hauz Rani village in New Delhi by the artist, autorickshaw drivers, community persons and volunteers

23 The Chiapas Photography Project, *Untitled*, by Xunka' López Díaz, 2000, from the book *Mi hermanita Cristina, una niña chamula/My Little Sister Cristina, a Chamula Girl*, by Xunka' López Díaz, 2000

24 Dilomprizulike, *Face of the City 1*, 2006, mixed media/installation

27

APPALSHOP

Learning from Rural Youth Media

Maritza Bautista

> What is the difference between how people see their own place and how others represent it? Who does get to tell the community story and what are the storytellers' responsibilities?
>
> Elizabeth Barret, *Stranger with a Camera*, 2000

For the past 40 years there has been ongoing dialogue, analysis, and mobilization in the heart of southeastern Kentucky through the work of Appalshop, one of the oldest media arts centers in the United States. Initially supported by funds made available through President Johnson's War on Poverty legislation, Appalshop set in motion an opportunity for rural youth to gain filmmaking skills. The youth took ownership of the program and continued to use filmmaking to address Appalachian issues with their own voices and confront stereotypical representations (see Plate 21).

I visited Appalshop back in 2008 with a group from south Texas as part of a program called Rural Filmmakers Exchange (RFE) designed by Hecho en Encinal and Appalshop to share and create new ideas about youth media arts. Hecho was about to launch Media del Monte (MdM), a six-week youth media summer program modeled after Appalshop's Appalachian Media Institute (AMI), and wanted to capture final ideas and methodologies used by AMI facilitators to guide us in the kick-off. In four days I participated in screenings and discussions of Appalshop/AMI films, videos and audio with youth and filmmakers, learned how to flatfoot dance and hiked on Pine Mountain where the hums of 17-year cicadas were ubiquitous.

When RFE ended, it was exciting to have procured Appalshop films because they would illustrate to MdM participants, as tools of cultural production, how to challenge issues critically. However, the relevance of rural Appalachia was not

114   Maritza Bautista

Appalshop, Rick DiClemente filming Dewey Thompson for the documentary *Chairmaker*, 1975, 16 mm color film (running time 22 minutes)

apparent to youth in rural south Texas. The youth in Encinal felt distanced by the Appalachian accent and were perplexed at why we would show them those films. The crossovers of the rural experience were present, but the MdM youth wanted to watch films they could better relate to and sought out the language and cultural experiences they knew. Nonetheless, the clear differences triggered an opportunity to engage in dialogue about how best to consider issues in rural south Texas knowing those stories would be then shared with others; they had to consider audience and distribution. Appalshop encapsulates the meaningful and transformative principles of exploring unique cultural, political, and economic conditions within specific communities.

Today, Appalshop continues to be a dynamic space that offers empowering media arts education and programming that promotes community collaboration while critically and justly preserving and representing cultural traditions of the rural mountain region. It exemplifies through its work that isolated communities have unique voices and particular stories are best told and challenged by the people who live them.

References

Barret, E. (Director). (2000). *Stranger with a camera* [Motion picture]. Whitesburg, KY: Appalshop.

28

NAVJOT ALTAF

What Public, Whose Art?

Manisha Sharma

Traveling verses of traditional wisdom; cheeky slogans on life, love, politics, ethics: visual samples of local culture bombard me as I crawl, speed, sit through Indian roads. Sample these translations: "my India is great but her public is troubled."[1] "An inebriate has two homes: the pub and the lockup."[2] South Asian transportation enthusiastically endorses the idea of bumper stickers as decorative declarations of personal and cultural beliefs. Buses, trucks, three-wheeler taxis (autorickshaws) are liberally adorned with stickers and hand-painted signs. These publicly made personal commentaries, these pithy poetics engage me with their often-local, sometimes-global social issues via our mutual movement through physical space.

Are these messages art or the autorickshaws; are the cab drivers artists in their image/meaning making? I wonder, thinking of their depictions in various graphic arts/photography/tourism books.

Indian artist Navjot Altaf invites us to consider the performance of this movement of and engagement with ideas across public spaces, as public art. *Autorickshaws* transforms silent consumption into interactive, multi-perspective conversations where we reflect on whose messages are being carried, whose stories told. Altaf questions the significance of the migration of people and stories and the role of those who enable these stories to travel. She meaningfully explores the identities of the "public" in "public art."

Altaf's work is layered, thoughtful; her process is art as much as the product. *Autorickshaws* is part of a larger project titled *Delhi Loves Me?* (see Plate 22) questioning how urban spaces acknowledge silenced populations. This includes migrant workers and their relationship with these spaces. In the first stage of the project, Altaf engages autorickshaw drivers of one community—an artists' village in New Delhi—in dialogue on these issues to create 15 stickers encapsulating this dialogue. Next she approaches the city's auto drivers, engaging them in the

Navjot Altaf 117

Navjot Altaf, *Delhi Loves Me?* (detail), 2005, sticker, 30 × 12 cm

discussion by asking them to carry these messages on their vehicles. The third stage takes it further when a video installation outside the artist village invites the general public to this dialogue of making, questioning, doubting, understanding, empowering, and sharing.

This, like most of Altaf's work, is an engagement with community to discuss how we make, consume, experience public art, and how process becomes art. It offers a wealth of inspiration in classroom discussions around social justice since it troubles issues of migration, urbanization, environment, access to ideas and expression, and the re-visioning of the form, function, and aesthetic of art in the developing (neocolonial) world.

The specificity of the form and setting of Altaf's work encourages us to eavesdrop on conversations of contemporary Indian art and society and to replenish clichéd caches of multicultural art education; however, the key themes in her work are of global concern and relevance and have larger resonance. Altaf's work offers artist educators new perspectives and vocabulary with which to engage in meaningful and lively conversations about art, education and justice. (At the very least, it may come in handy if South-Asian-American month is introduced in the curriculum.)

Notes

1 Original Hindi text: *Mera bharat mahaan, magar public pareshan.*
2 Original Hindi text: *Sharaabi kay do hi thikaanay, thekay jaaiay ya thaanay.*

29

THE CHIAPAS PHOTOGRAPHY PROJECT

You Can't Unsee It

Lisa Yun Lee

> The trouble is that once you see it, you can't unsee it. And once you've seen it, keeping quiet, saying nothing, becomes as political an act as speaking out.
> Arundhati Roy, 2002, p. 7

How does a photograph of brilliantly colored heirloom chili peppers, or hands shaping tortillas in a traditional manner express the desire for food, work, land, justice, and dignity? And how can the simple gesture of looking at these photographs become an act of resistance?

The Chiapas Photography Project, an archive by and for indigenous photographers, includes images that lovingly document traditional foods, ways of life, and people (see Plate 23). Indigenous people maintain to some degree distinct cultural, organizational and/or linguistic characteristics from the dominant culture of the nation state that often contests their cultural sovereignty and their right to self-determination. There is an ideological danger to romanticizing the idea of the indigenous in a way that echoes of racist representations of the "Noble Savage." Pretending that there is an idyllic existence removed from the conflicts that define the modern world fails to acknowledge that the right to remain faithful to a traditional way of life in modern times includes the struggle against capitalist agriculture and a competition for limited resources in a global economy. Chiapas is the region in Mexico where the Zapatistas have staked out their territory for resistance. The Zapatista Army of National Liberation (Ejército Zapatista de Liberación Nacional, EZLN) does not demand independence from Mexico, but rather autonomy, asking (among other things) that the natural resources extracted from Chiapas benefit more directly the people of Chiapas. Cultural sovereignty and the right to self-determination are political struggles that are not advanced by romantic fantasies.

120 Lisa Yun Lee

The Chiapas Photography Project, Emiliano Guzmán Meza, *Untitled*, 2000, from the book *Ixim/Maíz/Corn* by Emiliano Guzmán Meza, 2004

The engaging photographs in the project are hopeful and exuberant in a way that is somewhat unexpected, but never naïve or romantic. Too often, photographs that document political and economic struggles are characterized by a wretched, dour aesthetic. Jacob Riis pioneered this type of photojournalism in his classic work *How the Other Half Lives: Studies Among the Tenements of New York* (1890). Riis blamed the apathy of the wealthier classes for the conditions of the tenement slums. He believed his photographs depicting the horrors of abject poverty would compel those in power and privilege to action. But there is an essential tension that critics such as Susan Sontag have named between the consumption of documentary photography and moral action. Sontag called this the "chronic voyeuristic relation" that we have to looking at the world through images, which too often fosters an attitude of anti-intervention.

So what impact do the images from the Chiapas Photography Project of indigenous life have for those like myself, living in an affluent mass-media society? The project not only documents indigenous ways of life, but the images convey joy and the right to the simple pleasures of life, whether it is appropriating a bucket for the purpose of washing one's hair, enjoying the shade under a tree next to our home, or playing in the streets with a friend. In this way, the photographs facilitate a moment of recognition in the shared and common right to self-determination and to existence. The images do not arouse the feeling that one should do something *for* the indigenous people of Chiapas, but rather a sense of solidarity and the desire to resolve the enormous disparity between things as they are and as what we believe they could and should be—for all of us.

References

Riis, J. A. (1890). *How the other half lives: Studies among the tenements of New York*. New York: Charles Scribner's Sons.

Roy, A. (2002). *Power politics*. Cambridge: South End Press.

30
DILOMPRIZULIKE
Art as Political Agency

Raimundo Martins

Dilomprizulike is an artist from Nigeria who creates art from discarded items and works under the name "The Junkman from Afrika."[1] His art, an enigmatic mixture of sculpture, assemblage and installation, unveils the scary, the ugly, strange faces of cities depreciated by values worthless, disguised in poor surroundings. It is an ideological narrative depicting the frustrations of disowned inhabitants of these cities; the agitation, the overflowing, and mainly, the overwhelming drama that characterizes common people daily's life. Dilomprizulike's studio in Lagos is "The Junkyard,"[2] an open space where he lives, runs an art centre for young artists and collects discarded materials: iron and steel scraps, odd aluminum pieces, rusted metal, wire, leather, rags, used utensils—remains and wastes of the consuming society (see Plate 24).

Permeated with a critical sensibility founded in a performative art conception, his work articulates the "political" as a conflict dimension that constitutes human societies. It goes beyond conventional practices of representation and criticism searching for art as political agency. In his works, the political belongs to a domain where social life is structured as practices and institutions through which human beings organize daily life. Paradoxically, this conception of political offers an inventive individualism that takes diversity and multiplicity as a starting point to promote cultural interventions as relevant artistic practices.

His sculptures/installations are live images telling life histories, aspirations, failures, and discriminations that sometimes our eyes are not capable of seeing and hearing. In contemporary culture, art works voice a political criticism of power since the relationships between art, image, and power present themselves with camouflage, subtlety, almost unperceivable. This political perspective is an artistic metaphor of common/public spaces inhabited by humans as living sculptures animated by voices and subjectivities. Dilomprizulike's art points out inequality, economic, social, and educational breaches present in Nigerian/African societies.

His work recovers a memory of the cities and the self-esteem of disowned people living in peripheral communities, helping them capture and recreate their meanings to understand collapses and transformations in these spaces. It is a synthesis of inter-relationships that are translated into art exhibitions at the same time that they spill onto social life searching for an awareness to reassign life to those living in the margins.

An educative aspect preponderant in Dilomprizulike's art is the emphasis in the notion that a political comprehension of artistic experience does not base itself in individual valuations or judgments, but in the plurality of analytical perspectives regarding art's objects and subjects and their social experiences of the visual.

Ambiguity and ambivalence are traces of Dilomprizulike's artistic production that allows different interpretations and may lead visitors, students, and art educators to manifest opposite or contradictory reactions and feelings. Such works can be seen as converging axes of re-signified narratives that concentrate important moral and political conflicts, economic, social, and ethical dilemmas as resources to teach, research, and practice art education.

In a political approach to art, one must not deal only with aesthetic problems or artistic concerns, but with facts and social realities that make possible discussions on culture, society, and their subjects.

Notes

1   www.servinghistory.com/topics/Dilomprizulike
2   http://thejunkyardafrika.net/index.html

31

IN SEARCH OF CLEAN WATER AND CRITICAL ENVIRONMENTAL JUSTICE

Collaborative Artistic Responses Through the Possibilities of Sustainability and Appropriate Technologies

B. Stephen Carpenter, II and Marissa Muñoz

Water is life. Worldwide, increasing demand for water by industry and agriculture far exceeds the amount people consume for daily survival. Whereas water was once considered part of a community commons, scarcity has motivated its corporate privatization. Potable water is increasingly available only to those who can afford it, and dangerously unavailable to those who cannot. As a result, a small portion of the world's population can afford the luxury of indoor plumbing and seemingly unlimited supplies of potable water in their homes, while millions of people are left without the means or access to safe drinking water in their communities. In discussing these global water shortages, there seem to be three distinct approaches: water discussed as a legally enforceable universal human right, water as a commoditized resource protected by monetary value in the free market, and water as a grassroots human rights issue addressed through non-formal pedagogy (Muñoz, 2010).

This chapter is a critical conversation between non-hierarchical collaborators. Our conversation models a generative approach to considering possibilities in response to/with/through the contexts of commons. More specifically, this chapter is a dialogic exchange about what educators, artists, and cultural workers can do, and are doing, to engage meaningful and sustainable responses to environmental injustice. Because such an undertaking is quite broad, here we focus specifically on the global water crisis of inequitable and inadequate access to potable water. We draw upon scholarship from various disciplines including sociology,

Clean Water and Critical Environmental Justice 125

Water Filter Production Demonstration as Public Pedagogy. Texas A&M University, 2007

cultural studies, curriculum studies, visual culture, and the arts as we construct interpretations of, and curriculum possibilities inspired by, the work of artists, educators, activists, and cultural workers. We offer the work of contemporary artists Mel Chin and Natalie Jeremijenko as two examples of individuals whose interdisciplinary artistic efforts for social justice embody the kinds of collaborative responses and public pedagogy we believe should be at the heart of current and future P-16 art and general education.

Steve: For the past few years we have both been concerned with the complexities of balancing scholarship and practical action as sustainable responses to environmental injustice. Our work with point-of-use ceramic water filters is a direct response to the global water crisis, and the subject of much of our work separately and collaboratively (Carpenter, 2010; Carpenter et al., 2009, 2010; Hoyt & Carpenter, 2008; Muñoz, 2010). The filters are porous vessels created from a mixture of local clay, combustible materials, and colloidal silver (a natural antimicrobial that combats waterborne diseases) inspired by the work of Potters for Peace (2010) and FilterPure (2010). Our inspiration came from the hard work of community activists, cultural change agents, and artists whose individual and combined efforts in communities around the world inspired us to respond to similar needs in the Texas border communities along the Rio Grande. Following the philosophy of "appropriate technology" advocated by artist, humanitarian, and water justice colleague Manny Hernandez (2001), we consciously use indigenous materials and resources to create the filters. By using appropriate technologies to keep the production costs low and the manufacture process sustainable; communities are enriched by improved health, quality of life, and the means to ensure continued access to clean drinking water. Our belief that water is a universal human right regardless of economic means has shaped our collaborative work with local residents, and has offered a viable plan for success where other approaches have failed.[1]

Marissa: In choosing to take action, our partnership has generated new extensions and collaborations while enriching the work at multiple levels. From the clay in our hands, to the concepts we communicate, to interpersonal relationships, and community development, each action contributes to the basic human right to clean water. In so doing, we echo Freire's *conscientization*, or transformative awakening, and grow from passive observers into active agents who create real-world critical interventions (Freire, 1998). This approach encourages learning by doing, responding, interacting, interrupting, and resisting a dominant culture that cultivates passivity, instead, embodying a pedagogy of "critical thinking that refuses to decouple education from democracy, politics from pedagogy, and understanding from public intervention" (Giroux, 2010, p. 492).

Scholars such as Peter Gleick (1999, 2000, 2006) focus on water and explore issues of politics and economics from a conservation perspective, suggesting place-based solutions and environmental justice. Gleick notes,

> An estimated 14–30 thousand people, mostly young children and the elderly, die every day from water-related diseases. At any given moment, approximately one half of the people in the developing world suffer from disease caused by drinking contaminated water or eating contaminated food.
>
> *(1999, p. 488)*

These people are not hypothetical but are real people who live near to where we live, with limited or no access to healthy potable water. When viable and simple solutions exist, remaining passive seems inhumane. Within our common contexts, water justice work embodies a praxis of teaching toward positive change as a critical intervention that directly addresses the reality of water inequality.

Water justice colleague and artist Richard Wukich explains,

> If I could teach people how to clean their water and have 10,999 children die a day instead of 11,000, I would feel like I accomplished something. It does not sound like a big statistic, but when it's your child, [one] becomes significant.
>
> *(Reyes, 2006)*

While many water studies often focus on statistics, water justice work begins with and centers around people focused on actions to make improvements. The kind of work Wukich and others like him perform is situated at the intersection of critical pedagogy and environmental justice, but creates customized solutions from a place-based, public pedagogy perspective. In order to more clearly describe the struggle toward water equity, I developed the concept of a *praxis of critical environmental justice*. Modeled after eco-justice pedagogy (Bowers, 2002), critical environmental justice facilitates critical interventions to respond to common contexts, based on:

1. **A non-hierarchal approach**, in both internal organizational structure and external community partnership models,
2. **Recognition of indigenous culture and knowledge**, using strength-based and culturally-relevant approaches,
3. **A recovery of the community commons**, including non-commoditized aspects of public health, advocacy, and community empowerment, and

4. **A sustainable ecology for future generations**, nurturing the next generation, and minimizes its ecological footprint.

Steve: This praxis of critical environmental justice seems to function as a framework to assess the kind of work we believe needs to be done. The work of several artists come to mind for me that seem to embody the kind of work outlined through your criteria of critical environmental justice. Specifically, the work of Mel Chin and Natalie Jeremijenko embody these criteria, but there are many others who also fit this description. "Revival Field" by Mel Chin is an environmental installation that takes on the responsibility of ecological restoration through the use of hyperaccumulator plants that treat contaminated soil by removing heavy metals. This work, while evident in all four of your criteria, seems to emphasize the contexts of the recovery of community commons and a sustainable ecology for future generations.

Natalie Jeremijenko's work is situated at the intersections of visual art, public pedagogy, technology, and environmental justice. Her most recent project is an interdisciplinary collaborative called the *xClinic*, an environmental health clinic and lab that provides visitors ("impatients") with prescriptions ("solutions") to respond to specific deficiencies in the environmental health of their communities. In a discussion of her work that includes responses to environmental injustices committed by industry, Jeremijenko asks two key questions: (1) "What is the opportunity for change that new media technologies present?" and (2) "How might we [seize that or] use that to [kind of] build the social change we want?" (*Daily Motion* 2010). These questions, like many of her projects, refer to all four of the criteria of critical environmental justice, but especially those that emphasize non-hierarchal approaches and the recovery of the community commons. Jeremijenko's interest in how technologies can encourage positive social change is a key link to the work of Chin and other artists who move beyond activism and into the realm of action to ensure a sustainable ecology for future generations.[2]

I see the examples of Chin, Jeremijenko, and our water filter work as inspiration for P-16 art and general education curriculum and praxis. In saying that, I am not necessarily suggesting that art and general education curricula mimic them precisely but rather use these examples as conceptual exemplars to serve as motivation for developing and enacting collaborative educational experiences that respond directly to social and environmental injustice. By placing an emphasis on sustainability and appropriate technologies, such curricula require educators and learners to consider all four contexts of critical environmental justice. In short, the contexts of critical environmental justice you outline can be used to inspire rather than prescribe positive change.

Marissa: There seems to be a common urgency to respond, whether for educators, artists, or community advocates. To prescribe would limit the generative possibilities unique to each place and collection of collaborators. However, by centering the learning experience around a collective response to a shared context, learners may experience the empowerment of affecting positive change in their own lives and communities, and in so doing, embody positive social change.

References

Bowers, C. A. (2002). Toward an eco-justice pedagogy. *Environmental Education Research*, 8(1), 21–34.

Carpenter, B. S. (2010). Embodied social justice: Water filter workshops as public pedagogy. In J. Sandlin, B. Schultz, & J. Burdick (Eds.), *Handbook of public pedagogy: Education and learning beyond schooling* (pp. 337–340). New York: Routledge.

Carpenter, B. S., Cornelius, A., Muñoz, M., & Sherow, E. (2009). (Re)considering public pedagogy in/as art education: Engaging social justice and place-based education. *Trends*, 31–36.

Carpenter, B. S., Taylor, P. G., & Cho, M. (2010). Making a (visual/visible) difference because people matter: Responsible artists and artistic responses to community. In T. Anderson, D. Gussak, K. K. Hallmark, & A. Paul (Eds.), *Art education working for social justice* (pp. 60–66). Reston, VA: National Art Education Association.

Daily Motion (2010). *Natalie Jeremijenko "Lifestyle experiments and the crisis of agency"*. Retrieved July 5, 2010 from www.dailymotion.com/video/x9vep2_natalie-jeremijenko-lifestyle-exper_tech

FilterPure (2010). *FilterPure: Providing safe drinking water for the underserved*. Retrieved September 23, 2010 from www.filterpurefilters.org/

Freire, P. (1998). *The Paulo Freire reader*. A. M. A. Freire & D. P. Macedo (Eds.), New York: Continuum International Publishing Group.

Giroux, H. (2010). Neoliberalism as public pedagogy. In J. Sandlin, B. Schultz & J. Burdick (Eds.), *Handbook of public pedagogy: Education and learning beyond schooling* (pp. 486–499). New York: Routledge.

Gleick, P. H. (1999). The human right to water. *Water Policy*, 1(5), 487–503.

Gleick, P. H. (2000). The changing water paradigm: A look at twenty-first century water resources development. *Water International*, 25(1), 127–138.

Gleick, P. H. (2006). Implementing the human right to water. In E. Riedel & P. Rothen (Eds.) *The Human Right to Water* (pp. 143–147). Berlin: BWV Berliner Wissenschafts-Verlag.

Hernandez, M. (2001). Appropriate technology in developing countries. *Evolving Legacies: The NCECA Journal 2001, 22*, 96–102.

Hoyt, M. W., & Carpenter, B. S. (2008). Navigating water/democracy: Thirst, irrigate, drown, cleanse. In A. Fidyk, J. Wallin, & K. den Heyer (Eds.), *Democratizing educational experience: Envisioning, embodying, enacting* (pp. 61–82). Troy, NY: Educators International Press.

Muñoz, M. (2010). The TAMU water project: Critical environmental justice as pedagogy. (Unpublished master's thesis.) Texas A&M University, College Station, TX.

Potters for Peace (2010). *Potters for peace.* Retrieved September 23, 2010 from http://s189535770.onlinehome.us/pottersforpeace/

Reyes, E. (2006). Colloidal silver combats water problems in Iraq. Retrieved November 3, 2009 from www.utopiasilver.com/emailtemp/articlepages/silverfiltersiraq.htm

Notes

1 For more information about our water project visit http://tamuwaterproject.wordpress.com/
2 For more information about Revival Field visit www.pbs.org/art21/artists/chin/clip2.html. For more information about xClinic visit www.environmentalhealthclinic.net/

32

OPENING SPACES FOR SUBJECTIVITY IN AN URBAN MIDDLE-SCHOOL ART CLASSROOM

A Dialogue between Theory and Practice

Carol Culp and Rubén Gaztambide-Fernández

In this dialogue between two teachers, the authors speak from their particular relationship to art education. Carol is a public middle-school teacher in Toronto and a graduate student at the Ontario Institute for Studies in Education (OISE). The chapter opens with a short description of Carol's work. This reflection is followed by a response from Rubén, a faculty member at OISE, in which he notes the challenges that Carol's experiences illustrate.

Carol Culp (CC): I teach art in a multi-ethnic, lower-income middle school in Scarborough, Ontario. Over time I became frustrated with my students' focus on being "good" at art and decided to ask students to investigate themselves as a subject. I hoped the students would start thinking about what was important to them without worrying too much about technique. We began with self-portraits. I gave lessons on the proportions of the human face and how to mix and apply acrylic paint. I gave students magazines and asked them to incorporate collage elements. I showed the students traditional, painted portraits from the National Portrait Gallery in London. The resulting projects were fairly predictable—faces looking directly at the viewer, some magazine pictures pasted on top. While the students liked their results, I felt let down. I wished that the students had gone a bit "deeper" and investigated themselves in more "meaningful" ways. I realized I had to stop and examine what I was doing. I had asked students to investigate themselves by looking at images painted by European "masters." I had asked them to create collages of "themselves" using images from mainstream magazines. Who was I investigating, the students or myself? What did I expect them to learn from this exercise? As one student pointed out, the portraits I had shown them were all about rich, old, dead people. I decided to use art forms from outside the "traditional" art world. One of the projects involved the creation of artist trading cards. I thought this project would allow students to use what I imagined to be their youth culture in their work.

Rubén Gaztambide-Fernández (RGF): Your reflection points to three moves that are critical for art educators committed to approaching their work through a social justice lens. First, you make a significant move from object to subject. Traditional art education is "object"-centered; it tends to place the "art work" over experiences with art and the relationships that shape those experiences. This manifests in the work art teachers do, such as the focus on technique over subject matter, the focus on the art objects as opposed to the context that makes the objects knowable as art, and the relationships that produce the experiences that can be had with an object. The move from object to subject involves what you describe as students investigating themselves as subjects and a focus on ideas rather than technique. Second, you make a move toward self-awareness and you offer a critique of your own investments, desires, and hopes. As teachers, we do what we do because we are moved by our views of what is worth knowing or experiencing, but we rarely expose what these are or where they come from. You are candid about how your desires manifest in what you do with your students, and that is a risky but crucial aspect of social justice work. The third move is that you recognize the importance of dealing deliberately with institutional demands. Often, recognizing these limitations marks the end of conversations about social justice, but you take these as things that simply delineate, but don't define your work, and you tackle the challenge of dealing with them without sacrificing your commitments to a justice oriented art education.

CC: Where moving from subject to object becomes problematic is that there is always an object that results, and this produces institutional expectations —I have to grade it, critique it, use the language of the curriculum documents to describe it, and there is an unsaid expectation from colleagues that the outcome has to be attractive. The other challenge is in requiring 12- and 13-year-olds to reveal themselves as subjects. This requires a kind of introspection that they are not usually asked to do. They end up guessing what I want. However, there are instances when a kid does something surprising. I worry about rewarding this appearance of going deeper with better grades or even my reactions. By rewarding them, it also becomes my triumph—*my* A student. When students reveal something about themselves, that is not my triumph, it's theirs.

RGF: It is interesting, this reluctance to take credit for an apparent success. When a student does work, and s/he says that it has been transformational, or s/he says thank you, often my reaction is, "well, I had nothing to do with it." We want to acknowledge that it is the student's process, but there is also the reluctance to take credit for setting up the conditions for something to happen, maybe even for learning to happen! Surely it is not our responsibility to ensure that something happens, and surely we can't predict or guarantee that something is going to happen, or that it has anything to do with what I hope will happen.

CC: This leads to the other side of the coin, in terms of the object. Students want to know how to make things that are appealing in their world. They wanted to learn about the proportions of the human face. Technique is not a requirement, but it's also not thrown away. If they draw a beautiful face, fantastic, but what does that even mean? Some students don't draw at all in the program, and that is fine. They don't have to paint. They just have to explain why they chose to do what they chose to do. I also have to respect that I can have all these ideas, but the students don't necessarily, and they do have expectations about what an art class is supposed to look like, and what an A looks like, or a B, and sometimes it takes a long time for them, for anyone, for me! I am still trying to figure it out. What's the purpose of the art class?

RGF: There is a difference between art education that seeks to build on prior knowledge and techniques removed from context, and art education that focuses on cultural production, in which the student is the one who has a vision and wants to learn, and to ask: how do I draw a face that looks realistic, because that is what I envision? Yet, we can't really know what our students envision, because communicating that vision involves an imperfect process of translation that is always already a failure. How can we comprehend a student's vision in a way that doesn't already fail to know that vision? When we fail to understand their vision, it is hard to fight against the notion that it is the student who lacks. For example, we have our own ideas of what it means to be self-reflective, and students are struggling to figure out what that is, because at the end of the day we are the ones giving them a grade, yet we don't want to impose a vision. That is why sometimes they end up producing these clichés, because as you said, they are trying to figure out what it is that we as teachers want from them. But this is the paradox: how do we avoid the clichés while insisting that we don't know what will come out of the process?

CC: With the self-portrait it was hard. In that way it was unsuccessful. In another way it was successful because most of the students were happy with their results, they wanted to share them, even if they seemed like clichés to me. But I thought the artist trading cards pushed the expectations. I told the students, "this is the card, you do what you want with it. I am very open to whatever you hand in to me." Interestingly, they did research them. They all went to Google and searched for artist trading cards, and I did get some that looked very much like what they saw online. But the ones who didn't go online tended to hand in things that you might not include in an art class, like sports cards, or the ones that were really trying to push my boundaries with swearing on them, for example.

RGF: This is interesting also in relationship to something you talk about. When we expose students to certain traditions of European art, the assumption is often that inner-city kids do not have art around them. In fact, they have lots of art around them. Just because they don't go to museums on a regular basis doesn't mean they don't have ideas about what art is; they have lots of ideas about art. They are surrounded by street art and they have access to so much technology that exposes them to visual culture, whether they think of it as art or not.

CC: It reminds me of a game we had on the interactive whiteboard, where you matched an image of a work with the artist. An Andy Warhol piece came up, and a kid said, "I have that T-shirt!" It's interesting that the assumptions that I have of my students and what they see in their youth culture are often stereotypical. I didn't take into account how many of my students grow up in very traditional religious homes, where the visual culture around them is not what I imagined, it's not the graffiti, it's not the trading cards, it's very different. There was one portrait I got that looked very much like a piece of tapestry, it looked like a mehndi tapestry. It was not what I expected to be handed in.

RGF: Students have their own conceptions of what art is, based on their particular family background, so certain kinds of patterns might be framed as art in other social and cultural contexts. But this is not a sign that more dominant aspects of popular and visual culture are not a part of their life, but that perhaps they do not think of these as art. The ideas about art that many students—and many art teachers—bring to the classroom are in fact very traditional conceptions of art. The notion of visual culture may or may not make sense to students, particularly when they have something invested in keeping a clear boundary between the drudgery of schools and the joys of life outside of schools. We can't just simply ignore the ideas and expectations about art that students bring with them and try to replace them with our own, presumably better, concept of visual culture. That's a pedagogical error that reinforces the hierarchy between teacher and student. As teachers, we become personally invested in these concepts, in ways that may or may not resonate with the students, but we end up imposing them because we have invested ourselves as teachers with these concepts. Yet, social transformation requires personal transformation, and that sometimes means risking these personal investments and opening ourselves up for new possibilities and new ways of relating to one another.

CC: Which once again places a significant amount of risk at the teacher's feet. While new ways of working with students that are based on the ideals of social justice are the goal, they come in direct confrontation with the institutions in which these relationships are played out. The pressures of "standards-based" learning often do not allow enough time and latitude for change to occur organically. It is my hope that my professional fears won't stop my own transformation nor those of other educators engaged in teaching the arts with a commitment to social justice.

33

STORY DRAWINGS

Revisiting Personal Struggles, Empathizing with "Others"

Sharif Bey

Jessica recently enrolled in one of my graduate courses. She was an exemplary student—passionate, outspoken, and loved to engage in critical discussions about world events and contemporary art. Weeks later, after her first field experience in the city schools, she came to my office expressing her anxieties about working with diverse student populations. "I was afraid of saying the wrong things. I was sure I might offend someone by accident," she explained. This was Jessica's first experience working with students of color and she was extremely anxious about how she would fit in as a white teacher in a predominantly African-American and Hispanic elementary school. Fortunately she confided about her lack of preparedness and shared her discomfort with feeling out of place in an environment where most of the population (students and teachers alike) did not look, speak, or share similar life experiences as she. Through this realization Jessica began to critically re-examine her formative experiences—in and out of school.

The following spring, I attended a presentation where another young white female art teacher shared some of the challenges she faced upon taking the helm of a diverse urban art program. She exclaimed, "My art teacher training program did not prepare me for *this!*" While some pre-service teacher training programs make genuine efforts to integrate a diversity of cultural perspectives and related issues into their curriculum, this exposure tends to be remedial at best. Due to limited interactions with diverse student populations, many teacher candidates enter the classroom with anxieties about their abilities to connect with students or their respective histories. As a result they may not have the necessary confidence to use the art class as a platform for exploring issues of race, culture, or historical inequalities. National teaching standards expect teacher-training programs to produce critically reflective practitioners (National Council for Accreditation of Teacher Education, 2010) but in addition to reflecting on our teaching practices and formative education, we should also prepare our teacher candidates to collectively reflect on their experiences outside of the classroom.

We navigate identities by way of our intersecting histories, cultures, occupations, values, beliefs, and responsibilities. Despite the perceived similarities within our hegemonic communities, these intersecting dynamics are what distinguish us from one another. "Throughout our lives we are engaged at various levels in the process of identity formation, shuffling and prioritizing the facets of identity that we hold of ourselves and present to others" (Charland, 2010, p. 188). Through revisiting and reflecting on our own lived experiences we can better understand how our identities are formed in relation to others. My own identity as an educator is continually shaped by reflecting on my formative experiences as an African-American male in inner-city Pittsburgh in the 1980s, as I negotiate new aspects of my identity as, a husband/father, developing scholar, researcher, art teacher trainer, studio artist, and world traveler. Nieto (1998) tells us, "If students are to transcend their own cultural experience in order to understand the differences of others, they need to go through a process of reflection and critique of their cultures and those of others" (p. 15). This might include problematizing the challenges we all face as we adapt to or are isolated from various social orders. Rather than focusing exclusively on discussions of victimhood and prejudice, deconstructing the impact of xenophobia on our lived experiences offers possibilities for restoring social justice. Xenophobia is defined as fear and hatred of strangers or foreigners or of anything that is strange or foreign. Through the visual arts we can combat the oppressive structures that lead to our anxieties about others by first challenging notions difference within our own hegemonic communities.

For addressing issues of diversity with my pre-service art teachers I adopted a useful writing prompt from a former colleague, "A time when I was made to feel different . . ." This short essay assignment precedes a studio assignment, both of which consistently result in poignant dialogues ranging in topic from challenges associated with various social pressures including: growing up disabled, bi-racial, dyslexic, homosexual, Muslim—to being adopted or entering college as a non-traditional student or as a single parent. Through listening, reflecting, and articulating our respective stories we shape the meaning, significance, and connectedness of our experiences. But what role can story and image play in challenging notions of difference?

I made some modifications to this writing assignment by additionally requiring my students to revisit the visual aspects of their foretold stories. Carpenter (2004) tells us "Pictures and stories depend on each other and are often deeply connected. With encouragement from teachers, children can communicate simple and complex narratives about a variety of themes through their story drawings" (p. 4). After examining the use of images and symbols to convey heightened emotion and action in various forms of sequential art, I asked students to transform their stories into comic strips with limited text. Revisiting these experiences through art assignments can facilitate platforms for discussions about discrimination,

Emily Puccia Colasacco, *Fat Albert is Not a Compliment* (Excerpt), 2010, pen and found image, 9 × 12 in.

Justin Magnotta, *Poser*, 2010, digital media, 11 × 17 in.

hazing, bullying, and the perceived social hierarchies to which many of us fall victim in our formative years (Bitz, 2004).

In addition to constructively examining the images, symbols, texts, and metaphors associated with racial, cultural, or political oppression within contemporary art, we can also generate empathy for those who endure various forms of oppression by discussing our personal challenges. While all art teachers may not feel as though they can confidently mediate discussions involving complex and provocative issues like racism, sexism, and classism in the art class, we can offer assignments that evoke exchanges resulting from various lived social pressures. It can also compel us to generate images that connect to these lived pains. For example, through discussions/prompts/visualizations, teachers might give students an opportunity to create single images that represent their perseverance, struggles, or pains, and then they can work backward toward placing these images into a sequential context. Sharing their authentic stories can bring forth subjectivities and personal images that push the boundaries of overused symbols and clichés (peace symbols, power fists, broken hearts) that students otherwise use to generically represent their moments of adversity or triumph. In recent years, images of arm casts, pregnancy tests, broken ice skates, and "out of style" jeans evoked personal stories that later served as points of departure for examining historical injustices of collective groups.

In addition to discussing the economical use of imagery and effective use of symbolism in sequential art, I share the work of contemporary artists who use culturally and politically loaded images and objects as well. For example, contemporary artists Michael Ray Charles and Fred Wilson create modern contexts for interpreting whipping posts, show performers, domestic and pop-culture icons (The Pillsbury Dough Boy, Elvis), shackles, fried chicken, watermelons, basketball hoops, and switchblades along with their perceived baggage to make social statements about race, culture, and perception. These symbols have historically served a political purpose and are rooted in the history of slavery and racial stereotypes (Harris, 2003). By recontextualizing black stereotypical caricatures (Mammy, Sambo, Zip Coon) Charles attempts to make social statements about past and present constructions and receptions of African-Americans. Charles layers a variety of images and texts stemming from dated advertisements and popular media including: carnival and outlaw posters, runaway slave ads, and National Basketball Association and Walt Disney logos to offer commentary about white people's perception of African-Americans.

Multimedia installation artist, Fred Wilson, who is of African and Native American descent, poignantly juxtaposes objects associated with the oppression of African slaves and other under-represented ethnic groups with those historically associated with privileged. Wilson locates these authentic objects within existing museum collections, then creates new contexts for reinterpreting them through their relationship to one another. In addition to exploring his racial and cultural heritage, Wilson also considers the display and reception of objects and images through his vast experience as a professional museum educator (Walker, 2001). Wilson's studio and museum explorations simultaneously draw from his identity as a museum employee as well as an African-Native American. Understanding how various aspects of our identities can inform our studio practice is critical to interpreting Wilson's work.

If teachers and students focus on the implications of power and privileged when interpreting works of art, students can have meaningful exchanges about the historical roots of inequality. Artists like Charles and Wilson bring issues of identity and social justice to the forefront and visual culture education urges art educators to analyze the social power and constructs surrounding images (Duncum, 2002; Keifer-Boyd, Amburgy, & Knight, 2007). However, inexperienced and seasoned art teachers may both have difficulties introducing such artists and issues into pre-existing curricular agendas. Nieto (1998) suggests that we first work to build a sense of community through personal exchanges before embarking on the challenging and painful issues that affect collective groups. "The most powerful learning results when students work and struggle with one another, even if it is sometimes difficult and challenging" (Nieto, 1998, p. 15).

This is just one strategy art teachers can employ when laying the groundwork for authentic discussions involving works of contemporary art that address racial and cultural disparity or historical inequities in the classroom. Students can discover that there is a relationship between our personal struggles and those endured by others? Wei (1998) suggests, "Writing and drawing help improve students' thinking about their own lives and society" (p. 214). In addition to connecting the critical issues in our personal lives with those affecting others, students can examine the social power of the images and symbols they produce (Bitz, 2004; Wei, 1998). They might consider the way in which these images signify—politically, culturally, contextually—the importance of their chosen images to the story, or what/how images communicate about people or how people are perceived. Discussing how images and objects convey emotions and evoke conversation can be an entry point for examining the signification of those used by the aforementioned artists, which can serve as a bridge for connecting this content to the familiar world of our students.

References

Bitz, M. (2004). The comic book project: The lives of urban youth. *Art Education*, *57*(2), 33–39.

Carpenter, B. S. (2004). Telling stories through contemporary images. *Art Education*, *57*(2), 4–5.

Charland, W. (2010). African American youth and artist's identity: Cultural models and aspirational foreclosure. *Studies in Art Education*, *51*(2), 115–133.

Duncum, P. (2002). Visual culture art education: Why, what and how. *International Journal of Art and Design Education*, *21*(1), 14–23.

Harris, D. M. (2003). *Colored pictures: Race and visual representation*. Chapel Hill, NC: The University of North Carolina Press.

Keifer-Boyd, K., Amburgy, P. M., & Knight, W. B. (2007). Unpacking privilege: Memory, culture, gender, race, and power in visual culture. *Art Education, 60*(3), 19–24.

National Council for Accreditation of Teacher Education. (2010). *Standards*. Retrieved August 10, 2010 from www.ncate.org/standards

Nieto, S. (1998). Affirmation, solidarity and critique: Moving beyond tolerance in education. In E. Lee, D. Menkart, & M. Okazawa-Rey (Eds.), *Beyond heroes and holidays: A practical guide to K-12 anti-racist, multicultural education and staff development*. Washington, DC: Network of Educators on the Americas, pp. 7–17.

Walker, S. (2001). *Teaching meaning in art making*. Worcester, MA: Davis Publications.

Wei, D. (1998). Students' stories in action comics. In E. Lee, D. Menkart, & M. Okazawa-Rey (Eds.), *Beyond heroes and holidays: A practical guide to K-12 anti-racist, multicultural education and staff development*. Washington, DC: Network of Educators on the Americas, pp. 212–221.

PART IV
Voices of Teachers

INTRODUCTION

Art Matters

Graeme Sullivan

Art and Social Justice Education: Culture as Commons is organized around the important premise that "art matters." This means that making art, encountering art, and using art, is considered to be crucial in understanding how we learn to make sense of the rapidly changing world around us. Our homes, schools and the social groups we belong to are expanding visual and virtual networks that rapidly link us to communities and cultures across space and time. The bridge over these boundaries is an experience that is common to all ages: the practice of making things that matter. Individuals and groups with common interests make many things, and these public images, objects, and events express ideas that communicate shared values and beliefs. These are the practices that give shape to cultural identity. However, as Maura Nugent explains in her essay, *Holding the Camera*, the practice of making things that matter is also "terrifically messy." As the voices of Maura and the other teachers in this section of the text richly illustrate, it may be that the values, beliefs, and experiences of the teacher are not the same as those of the student. Therefore, to assist others to make things that matter is to acknowledge that making is also a private process that shapes the way we think, our relationships with others, and how our ideas become actions that can make a difference.

This text is based on three core principles dealing with *knowledge, cultural recognition* and *personal and social transformation*. The approach to knowledge is that it is a human right and education can provide a means for individuals to take ownership of the forms, ideas and actions that shape their understanding. A good example of this is the essay by William Estrada, *Animating the Bill of Rights*, where students begin by raising questions about some of the underlying assumptions found in the Pledge of Allegiance because they "feel that the pledge isn't a true representation of what they see in their communities or what they experience."

Graeme Sullivan, *Streetwalks: Inside LA III*, 2010, discarded timber frame, sheetrock, canvas, wire, 33 in. × 32.5 in. Archival digital prints by Ken Allen Studios, Brooklyn, New York. Worn in a public procession along Wilshire Boulevard commemorating the 1992 Los Angeles riots in Koreatown

Their response was to create an animated film whereby the editing processes allowed them to constantly critique the images and meanings being constructed within the critical pedagogical traditions of action research. This theme of informed action that comes from insights gained from working alongside others is consistent throughout the teachers' essays that follow. As Delaney Gersten Susie infers, knowledge is challenged and changed by creating opportunities for others to fully participate in the learning process: "I am just now realizing that teaching for social justice is less about what you do and more how you do it. To teach *with* justice."

Cultural recognition acknowledges that coming to know and appreciate what others "make" has the capacity to not only expand our understanding of the diversity of cultural practices, but also to tell us about ourselves. This goes hand in hand with the third theme, which emphasizes the social responsibility of artists and teachers in using art learning as a means of personal and social transformation. Each of these principles comes to life through the voices and visions of the teacher's accounts. In Bert Stabler's essay about teaching art in an inner-city public high school he connects the issue-laden aspect of contemporary art with the humanist tradition of individuality to "open up the possibility of students re-evaluating their own sense of power and their image of themselves as hopelessly marginalized non-citizens." Bert makes use of wider public art spaces and related political discourse to empower his students and to enliven the image of the neighborhood school as an active participant in the life of the community. Keith "K-Dub" Williams seeks a similar voice for his students whereby the streets and the community become the "canvas" for teaching and learning. In much the same way, the title of Vanessa López-Sparaco's essay, *Whatever Comes Next will be Made and Named by Us*, captures the pedagogical problem she confronts and the artistic solution she pursues for the diverse population of students she teaches.

In seeing art learning as a process of creating knowledge, a socially situated practice, and an individually and socially transformative process, these authors describe why art, social structures, and politics, are essential elements in contemporary art education. Within the art classroom in the school these educational components translate into curriculum issues about what art is taught, why art is important, and how art can be made meaningful to students, parents and the community. More specifically, for the classroom art teacher, decisions have to be made about the art content that is encountered and created, how responsive and inclusive it is to be, and the means by which the students can be encouraged to take ownership of their art learning.

The implication for art teachers is to consider how knowledge, relationships, and actions shape what happens in their art classrooms, and it is the idea that art is a creative and critical "research" practice that opens up new pedagogical possibilities. Although use of the term "research" is mostly found within university settings and across educational debates, at the heart of it, the purpose of research is to create knowledge that matters. This new knowledge not only builds on what we already know, but is also created from imaginative ideas and within creative spaces where unexpected outcomes may challenge and change what we don't know because this can profoundly change what we do know. This is what Anne Thulson describes in her essay, *Think Twice, Make Once*. The "expeditionary" learning of her middle schoolers uses art and science research as the context for site-based art projects that disrupt how knowledge is presented in the classroom and interrupt accepted public perceptions about local narratives. Anne adds:

> Our interaction was unexpected. The results were unknown. We experienced the disequilibrium of our uncertain roles with our viewers, the joy when people were moved by our efforts, an affinity with nature, and meaningful, unexpected dialogue with strangers about the untold story of the river.

The teachers' essays that follow have numerous references to the art practice undertaken in their classrooms as a research activity. Their descriptions identify approaches that are similar to how I describe art practice as research.

> The critical and creative investigations that occur in studios, galleries, on the Internet, in community spaces, and other places where artists work, are forms of research based on studio art practice. Rather than adopting methods of inquiry from the social sciences, the research practices explored subscribe to the view that similar research goals can be achieved by following different yet complementary paths. What is common is the attention to systematic inquiry, yet in a way that privileges the role imagination and intellect plays in constructing knowledge that is not only new but has the capacity to transform human understanding.
>
> (Sullivan, 2010, p. xix)

The arguments I make in this text and on the related website, www.artpracticeasresearch.com, bring together ideas from several sources. These include the incisive, probing eye of contemporary art, the critical edge of cultural practices, the capacity of universities to continually seek new knowledge, and the responsibility of schools to not only respond to the world as it is, but to also imagine it as it might be. This is the point that Zoe makes in her quote cited in Kimberly Lane's essay, where she echoes a quip Maxine Greene often makes in conversation, which is that art can't change the world but it can change someone who can. In discussing the social activist art of Luba Lukova in class, Zoe said:

> Her images are effective, even if they don't change any specific practice. The fact that we are learning about her message at school shows that her work is teaching future generations, those who will be able to make a change.

When the scope and responsiveness of art teaching meets the multimodal minds of young artist–researchers the rewards can be rich. As Jesse Senechal explains in his essay, *The Zine Teacher's Dilemma*, even if there is "uncertainty of definition" surrounding the art teacher's role, the openness that comes when authority is eased and experience is privileged can be the basis for sustained, inventive art action. The robust ideas, inventive processes, and purposeful use of creative and critical art practices evident in these teachers' accounts indicate that schools can be highly active, imaginative, life-changing places.

Reference

Sullivan, G. (2010). *Art practice as research: Inquiry in visual arts*. Thousand Oaks, CA: Sage.

34

HOLDING THE CAMERA

Maura Nugent

Chicago wind burns our ungloved hands as we grasp clipboards and video cameras. I remind my students, "What did we decide we need b-roll footage of? Condo signs, the Starbucks, Jimenez grocery store . . ." My voice fades as we come across a playground and my 15- and 16-year-old students take off running for the equipment, flinging themselves down the slides and belly flopping onto the swings, their laughter echoing across the empty playground. Off to the side, one of my students captures this gleeful frolicking with her video camera. I think about telling her to not waste the battery and film on this—but I resist the urge. It is not my job to hold the camera right now.

We are working on our research/documentary project—this particular one is about affordable housing. The project is one we've done for several years in the Kelvyn Park Social Justice Academy where I've taught for seven years. The documentary projects always begin with the question: what is the biggest injustice facing our community? This simple question spans almost an entire semester of work. The students begin first with an extensive process to collectively decide what injustice they want to focus on and then undertake a research project that involves reading, interviewing, writing, and field research, all while crafting a documentary on the topic, which they will eventually showcase in a large community forum. The film then can be used as a tool for continued work and organizing on the issue—thanks to a partnership with a local community based organization, the Logan Square Neighborhood Association. In the three years we have done this project, we've also enlisted the help of a video artist, Saya Hilman.

The project is terrifically messy, as I have come to believe all good art, education, and social justice work is. For one thing, we never know ahead of time what topic the students will settle on and so we have to craft the curriculum as we go. Inevitably, halfway through the project there is always a sense of the whole thing spinning out of control. Students and teachers alike become weary of the topic—and there is always the kid who moans, "Aren't we *done* talking about this?" We become lost in reading articles that no longer seem relevant to questions the kids are raising, we have hours of unexamined footage of interviews—not to mention hours of b-roll footage that we have not yet begun to sort through.

Ah, yes, the b-roll footage. The project requires many days of collecting the footage that will be shown interspersed with, and as background to, the interviews. As teachers we try to structure this as much as possible—brainstorming with the students what footage we need, getting permission to go into the neighborhood to film, putting the students into project groups in which each student has a distinct role, and enlisting the help of volunteers to work with the groups. All these are our efforts to control the chaos that is inevitable when one sends teenagers out into the world with video cameras. I often feel nervous as they head out to shoot b-roll, but the students are always gleefully confident. They seem filled with a sense of delicious power as the video camera goes into their hands and they are sent off to capture the world as they see it. Holding the camera puts them in charge. (Perhaps that is why I feel nervous.)

So, naturally, we end up with footage of their friends rapping for the camera, students chasing each other and yelling obscenities, close-up shots of the spicy hot wings served at lunch. Truly relevant images, no? During the most recent project, one of my co-teachers, Sean O'Bra, and I watched hours of this kind of footage, shaking our heads and asking: "Don't they know we're going to watch all this? Why are they capturing this nonsense?"

Such is the mindset of a teacher—which is why it's good we're not holding the camera. Because the truth is we don't always understand what needs to be captured. I love my students dearly, and try hard to understand the realities of their lives as I work in solidarity with them towards goals of social justice. But as a white, middle-class adult, I am on some level always an outsider to their world. And too often, outsiders get to "hold the camera" and represent what the Kelvyn Park community is: "inner-city school," "failing school," "dangerous neighborhood." Simplified, often inaccurate versions are constantly represented over and over again in the media. So many people who have never set foot inside an "inner-city failing school" accept these representations as truth. And the real danger is that impactful policy is made based on these representations.

So there is something powerful about handing a kid a video camera and telling them: *show me, show me what's important. Let's craft a work of art from your point of view*—*to show the world what they need to see.*

In part of the final documentary on housing the students read excerpts of their "I Am From" poems while images flash across the screen. The images are b-roll the students shot. It is spliced together in a vibrant tapestry of images—a wobbly panning image of Kelvyn Park as students spill out the door at the end of the day with their headphones and backpacks, graffiti on an empty condo building in mid-construction, the local grocery store with colorful signs in the window advertising the specials—cochinita, barbacoa, tamales, and carnitas—a man sleeping on a bench, a community meeting . . . and then there's that footage I thought was a waste—my "tough" teenagers joyfully climbing on playground equipment like little kids. This footage that I thought wasn't important wonderfully captures this complex, struggling, beautiful community of which my students are a part.

Good thing I wasn't holding the camera.

35

THE STREETS ARE OUR CANVAS

Skateboarding, Hip-Hop, and School

Keith "K-Dub" Williams

When one thinks of skateboarding today the image that comes to mind is Tony Hawk or a Southern California vibe and lifestyle. Although Tony Hawk is the modern-day icon, skateboarding culture has grown into a popular activity for many youth in our inner cities, in addition to popular mainstream influences of X-Games, MTV/Rob Drydek, video games, skate-themed apparel, hip-hop artists Pharrell, and Lupe Fiasco. Add also the development of skateparks being built now in urban areas and that skateboard culture has become a worldwide multi-million dollar industry.

In 2004, while teaching at Oakland High School in California I created a skateboard club after seeing a few students rolling around our campus. I've skated since "back in the day" growing up in south Los Angeles and I share a love of the sport with the new generation of urban skaters. Around that time I also began to notice more youth of color gravitating to skateboard culture, wearing the apparel and skateboarding around the city.

Then, I attended the world famous '04 X-Games in Los Angeles, and again noticed that the diversity of the crowd in attendance did not carry over into the competition. The following school year, I served as the Co-Director of Oakland High School's Visual Arts Academy and helped to create "Tha Hood Games" to give youth an opportunity to showcase their skateboarding talents in a predominately white sport that didn't feature events in urban areas. In short, Tha Hood Games was created to be everything that X-Games isn't.

I decided to use the Tha Hood Games as a way to teach my students how to use the community and streets as a "canvas." First, through connections I developed as a community muralist I gained access to a small parking lot at the East Oakland Youth Development Center (EOYDC) to host our first event in 2005. I also enlisted other clubs on Oakland High's campus—the hip-hop club provided student DJs and student performances, and the fashion club made

Graphic design by Ryan Espinosa, art direction by K-Dub, *Hood Games #1*, April 2005, Photoshop document, 5 × 7 in.

skater-themed outfits and thrilled the crowd with a dazzling student fashion show. My advanced art students and skateboard club members designed the event flyer, and made canvas artwork that adorned the surrounding parking lot fence. Professional skateboarder Karl Watson, an Oakland native whom I knew from K-Dub the X-Games, was given the task of inviting other pro skaters to attend the event, skate with the youth and share their skills in a relaxed vibe.

This became a real community event: a neighborhood skateboard shop provided skate ramps and obstacles for the day, and a local skateboard company gave me skateboards that I used as the basis for a class project—each student in my advanced art class designed her or his own limited edition skateboard deck. I wanted my students to feel included in every aspect of skateboarding culture from the design of the boards, to planning and participating in the event. Even my mother, Ms. Adjoa Murden, a retiree of Los Angeles Children's Social Services who had always supported my skating while I was growing up, got involved. Hood Games #1 was a great day—youth from all over the Bay Area came to east Oakland to the free skateboard event and joined in with local residents, pro skaters, and people from our school. Once the sweet sounds of positive reggae music filled the air, it was a gathering of cultures and community. Finally, our skating community was able to enjoy this activity locally instead of in another neighborhood or at a suburban skatepark.

The success of the first event led me to take the template to south Los Angeles during the summer of 2005 by reaching out to local youth groups and community centers. Again the event was a community success and again, pro skateboarders found their way into inner-city neighborhoods and skated with the youth.

I am an artist, but after these successes finding time to make my own art became secondary to the need to create more of these experiences, which rally local schools and youth centers to involve artists, athletes, musicians, and youth performers to share their talents in sometimes overlooked communities. Two things are for sure: these young skaters have been proud to share their talents within their community, and the community was ready to support a skateboard event.

To date, Tha Hood Games has produced 30 events in Oakland, San Francisco, Los Angeles, Long Beach, and Las Vegas communities and local parks, many skateboard-focused art exhibitions and three skateboard-themed film festivals. Three years ago X-Games created the Hood Games Xperience, which allows 35 youth from Los Angeles, Long Beach and Oakland to skate on the professional street course. It feels like I've come full circle: I created Tha Hood Games because I didn't see diversity on the big stage. By involving my students and other young people in creating a neighborhood event, I have helped to open up the sport's biggest arena to new populations of young people across the state.

I am now working as an art educator in a middle school. I like to share this story with my young students as an example of how an artist's work can be about more than just her or his own vision and personal goals; it can also include creating ways to benefit a whole community.

36

THE ZINE TEACHER'S DILEMMA

Jesse Senechal

Soon after I began teaching at Kelvyn Park High School in Chicago, two students from my English class approached to ask if I would sponsor a school publication for their art and poetry. I agreed and over the next few months we were able to collect a variety of student work, and then cut, paste, copy, and staple it into the first issue of *ROAR*. When I think back to 1996 and those early years of *ROAR*, the image that most often comes into my head is of the release day. A bell would ring at the end of a period and a sea of high-school students dressed in drab blue and white uniforms would spill into the halls and gather around the brightly colored covers of the magazine. There was excitement for me watching them stand in groups and flip quickly, then slowly, through the pages. I remember them pointing, talking, smiling, laughing, looking for their names, their friends' names, their words, and images, while ignoring the bells and security guards that were telling them "go where you belong!"

As the adviser for *ROAR* I was never exactly sure what it was. My original thought was literary magazine—one of those sanctioned school publications that highlight the most promising work of the most talented young writers and artists. However, *ROAR* quickly shifted away from that model in content and form into something that would more accurately be classified as a zine. The term zine (pronounced *zeen*) refers to a self-published magazine and is identified with a broad cultural movement that exploded in the early 1970s at the intersection of the punk rock DIY (do it yourself) philosophy and cheap consumer printing technologies (most notably, the copy machine). Like many zines, *ROAR* had an open rather than selective editorial policy, a small distribution (1000–2000 copies), a specific subculture focus (urban high-school Latino youth), no profit motives, and a devoted fan base. Yet, as much as I think of *ROAR* as a zine, I am hesitant to embrace that label fully. Part of this hesitation has to do with the

Jason Alforo, *ROAR #1*, April 1997, silkscreen, 8.5 × 11 in.

fact that when we published that first issue of *ROAR* in April of 1997, I knew little to nothing about the history or culture of the form. While I had seen zines around friends' houses and probably flipped through them, I had never collected or traded them and I had certainly never made one before. But my hesitation about calling *ROAR* a zine is not just about my initial ignorance. A larger part of it has to do with what I see as a fundamental paradox of *teaching* zine-making.

Many schools, especially urban schools, are systems built on rigid hierarchical structures of power and control. The metal detectors, bells, and drab uniforms are just a sign of the problem. At a more basic level, there are the roles played out within schools and the unavoidable relationships that emerge in this setting. A security guard, as good-natured as anyone might be, must still play the role, telling students, "go where you belong!" And as a teacher, as much as I might have wanted to encourage student voice and agency, I often had to act as the authority in the classroom—shaping curriculum, organizing seating arrangements, disciplining, and giving grades. Zine-making, in contrast to schooling, is based on a redistribution of authority (the authority to publish). While the explicit content of zines does not have to be political (although many are), the act of making a zine has a political significance. It's a reclaiming of power to those for whom the sanctioned forms of publication do not speak. So the paradox of *teaching* zine-making is, simply put, when you make a zine because your teacher told you to, then maybe it's not a zine at all. Although the idea for *ROAR* first emerged from the students, I was the one that kept it going through ten years and 24 issues. I was the one that recruited students each year, wrote the curriculum, and kept the vision focused. While through the years *ROAR* began looking more and more like a student zine (with interviews and rants and comics and other random cultural expressions by students), it was not, in practice, a fully student-led publication. There was always compromise. Student voice was important but the teacher's authority was never relinquished.

As *ROAR* became more of a zine and as I became more invested in it as a zine, the paradox of the pedagogical project became clearer to me. However, at a certain point, my feelings about this dilemma shifted from uncertainty to acceptance. Ultimately, I figured that the best thing to do was embrace the paradox and move forward. For while, on the one hand, it seemed somewhat problematic to teach a subversive act like zine-making from a position of authority, on the other, it made perfect sense to teach a subversive act like zine-making in the broader authoritarian context of school. What better place for it? I'm sure that Kelvyn Park was not unique in the fact that there was a rich base of student resistance from which to draw: doodles on tests, classroom graffiti, worn notebooks and sketchbooks of raps and comics, mix tapes, and homemade t-shirts. This creative impulse among students to publish in unsanctioned forms was the foundation on which *ROAR* was built. And while some might argue that creating an official outlet for these forms of publication is an act of co-opting, it seemed to me that *ROAR* created a space of freedom within the traditional school context that not only became a haven for many of the more subversive spirits, and helped make school a bearable experience, but also challenged the official culture and structures of the school. *ROAR* regularly pushed boundaries and often got in trouble with what was published, but they were boundaries that, in my opinion, needed to be pushed. They were generally boundaries that were based on the premise that students and their voices need to be controlled.

So while there remains uncertainty in my mind about whether a zine teacher can really teach zines, I am left with the sense that this uncertainty of definition is worth the rewards of doing it anyway.

37

MIRACLE ON 79TH STREET

Using Community as Curriculum

Delaney Gersten Susie

When I pull into the parking lot of my school I sometimes feel like I am in a spaceship flying in from another planet. The students watch as this alien who is also their art teacher gathers her bags and walks to the school building. I am a white woman, and my students are all African-American, and like so many new teachers in urban public schools, I am not from their neighborhood. I expected to cross a cultural divide when I started this job. As a white woman working in an all-black school and community, I expected that I might feel like an outsider. What surprised me was the realization in my second year that while the rest of the teaching staff seemed to me to be "insiders," many also live outside the community in which we teach. This dynamic is never explicitly talked about at our school, but it definitely affects learning, curriculum and relationships.

There are physical walls on a school but also metaphorical walls that keep out the community and everyday relevance from the learning happening inside. Often I worry, "How can I genuinely teach my students when I don't understand where they come from?" Since I have the overwhelming blessing of teaching art to all 630 of our elementary students, kindergarten to 8th grade, I am in a unique position to help bring the community and students' realities back into learning.

In my second year I had students use their neighborhood for inquiry and exploration in our art class. We were preparing for the school pageant "Miracle on 79th Street – Yes, I Believe!" Younger grades made maps about important everyday places. Older students drew the architecture commonly featured in the neighborhood. All classes brainstormed a list of "local landmarks—places that are important to you." I took a small group of 8th graders on a neighborhood tour to photograph these places to inspire mural paintings. They led the way. We left the familiar school grounds to meet the hustle of 79th Street, and captured the first local landmarks—Dorothy's Beauty Shop, 4 Brothers Liquors and Food, and

Miracle on 79th Street 161

Miracle on 79th Street, Scott Joplin School, Chicago, 2011

Pepe's Mexican fast food. We took pictures of nearby churches, the park, fire station, library, and more. Our neighborhood tour lasted until sunset, and I went home thankful for the lessons about the neighborhood these student ambassadors taught me.

The informal nature of the outing allowed genuine learning for both me and my students. They learned about photography and architecture—one girl learned that her house had a special name, a Chicago *bungalow*. I learned about my students by how they related to their surroundings. I realized that these students had never really considered their community's history or knew its name—Auburn Gresham. They called their neighborhood by their city block, and knew little about communities a few blocks away.

We all learned how to cross invisible boundaries around us. Students who had never traveled far from home discovered new places and I became more familiar with the community in which I teach. Some of my other students saw us and waved with a mixture of excitement and confusion. Interestingly, overall behavior in my classes improved after the neighborhood tour. Walking their streets, my students saw me as a real person, and I began to see them as whole people within the context of their community.

The culmination of this unit was the creation of 12 murals. The night of the pageant hundreds of people filled the gym, surrounded by images of the neighborhood as seen through the eyes of the children vibrating in colorful, heavy-handed paint strokes. I wished that every class had participated equally—I wasn't able to take every class on a neighborhood walk—and the depth of our critical conversations left me wanting more, but still, I felt I had managed to use the arts to bring the community inside the school.

The landmarks mural project provided a powerful way for my students and I to learn from each other. This simple act is often ignored in schools, causing some schools to become what Lisa Delpit (1995) describes as "institutions of isolation," in which teachers feel the need to remediate the deficiencies of culturally different students (p. 179). Delpit pinpoints the importance of appreciating our students' communities in the following passage:

> Nowhere do we foster inquiry into who our students really are or encourage teachers to develop links to the often rich home lives of students, yet teachers cannot hope to begin to understand who sits before them unless they can connect with families and communities from which their students come.
>
> *(p. 179)*

I am entering my 6th year teaching in elementary schools serving students of color affected by poverty, and I am just now realizing that teaching for social justice is less about what you do and more how you do it. To teach *with* justice requires more than a lesson plan. It requires examining prejudices and questioning notions of what or how we "should" be teaching. Teaching art in an elementary school is about fairness, critical thinking, community-building and free expression. My first year out of graduate school, I taught lessons for social justice that fell short because I didn't take the time to know my students and reflect honestly on my own assumptions. I wasn't always willing to alter my delivery or our topics of inquiry to meet my students' needs. I got mad when my students didn't get excited about my cutting-edge lessons, but stubbornly kept teaching them because I felt like the class deserved them. Reflecting on this, I learned that it is possible to teach social justice topics in a way that hinders justice for your students, and that learning your students is the most critical step in meaningful teaching.

References

Delpit, L. (1995). *Other people's children: Cultural conflict in the classroom.* New York: The New Press.

38

PUBLIC SCHOOL, PUBLIC FAILURE, PUBLIC ART?

Bert Stabler

In a public school, the context for every interaction is the state. And how do low-income, majority African-American communities know the state? Not as benign representatives, elected by consensus and providing needed services, but as a foreign power that pays police, builds prisons, and neglects and destroys public housing—as a despotic and ridiculous stranger. A required art course, in this kind of environment, has a crisis of purpose, and is thus a politically charged space. For most students, art is an empty hole in the school regime that exposes the institution's coercive nature. This crisis of purpose represents the intersection of two separate crises of purpose—that of contemporary fine art and that of humanist education. Deprived of credible necessity, art class becomes about power, a theater of inculcating and resisting arbitrary discipline.

I teach art in such a neighborhood high school, on Chicago's southeast side. My classroom is the spacious and well-lit former wood shop (a reminder of the area's deindustrialization), and I have always enjoyed a wonderful degree of freedom from my administration. It is a large high school with about 1500 students, divided into four "small schools"—one small school has three art teachers and gets most of the aspiring artists and designers; another school gets students with a strong technology bent, and the third school is oriented around health-care careers. I am the only art teacher in the fourth small school, which only allegedly emphasizes environmental studies.

The apathy and animosity I face in my students on a daily basis may be in some part a reaction to my teaching style, but I would attribute it more to my role in their lives—both as a teacher and as a white male authority figure. And I can't ignore that art, among the students I teach, is a subject mostly greeted with little enthusiasm or respect. Parents and guardians, equally distrustful and overwhelmed by numerous challenges, are involved with the school in only the

Public School, Public Failure, Public Art? 165

Solar Powered Inflatable Exotic and Endangered Species Project, created by students at Bowen Environmental Studies Team (B.E.S.T.) High School and demonstrated for students at Coles Elementary School, Chicago, 2010

most obligatory fashion. Few to none participate in our local school council, a small fraction show up for report card pickup day, and a common result of informing parents of a student's poor attendance, slipping grades, or problem behavior is a physical beating.

I primarily teach sophomores in my Art 1 classes, but I also work with seniors in an Advanced Placement (A.P.) Studio Art class. Since motivation is a major issue, I try to offer students service-learning credit along with course credit, and so I focus a great deal on projects that not only point to but have some existence in the world outside of school. Students have a great deal of flexibility in the product they make, but my materials budget ranges from limited to none, and I plan many projects based on grants I apply for or things I have left over or scrape up for free. I haven't had good luck with open-ended work, and so the concept is generally top-down and results are gauged based on a simple rubric of expectations. The flip side of this is that students have substantial autonomy in how they pace themselves and make formal decisions. Additionally, any student who wants to pursue an alternative direction, or even an alternative project, is entirely free to do so.

I have found various venues in which to present our research and creation to the larger world. We had a show of architectural drawings and proposals on Chicago's public housing at Mess Hall, a Chicago community art space. The Hyde Park Art Center hosted a show on textiles of the African Diaspora, for which students created and distributed a photocopied magazine. Mike Bancroft of Cooperative Image Group and I have collaborated using student artwork in guerrilla "interventions" to bring attention to homelessness, youth violence, and environmental racism. And a mosaic sculpture on economic justice is (unfortunately) still in progress in front of the school.

The best experiences happen when we get outside of the classroom. We made striking anti-violence posters with stencil, screen, and block prints, and had a great time attending a memorial for slain civilians in Iraq held by the Friends National Service Committee downtown. Students collaborated on a giant nightstick-wielding cardboard robot with a camera for a head that represented the link between prisons and schools, and much fun was had by the group that installed the robot at the Hyde Park Art Center. At the end of last year we teamed up with a prisoners' rights group known as Tamms Year Ten, who was advocating for the conviction of notorious Chicago police commander and torturer Jon Burge. We created embroidered patches with messages to sew on to prisoner uniforms, which were then worn by the Tamms members at a demonstration on the first day of Burge's trial. We got to go downtown and see the protest, which was a powerful experience, and one of our students was interviewed by a radio journalist.

This year students studied various Illinois wild animals of their choice. After we practiced blowing up plastic-bag assemblages with box fans and made smaller models from newspapers and tape, groups of students created large painted inflatable models of Illinois animals, which we blew up with leaf-blowers powered by a solar panel. Several of us got to go to an outdoor gathering at a local elementary school, and do a show and tell with young students, all about our animals, our art, and solar power. We will be continuing the environmental theme with a site-specific outdoor installation calling attention to toxic brownfields in the neighborhood.

All of these projects don't make art class any less political, but they might open up the possibility of students re-evaluating their own sense of power and their image of themselves as hopelessly marginalized non-citizens. Moving outside the boundaries of school relieves the sense of dread, resentment, and contempt associated with constrictive boredom, pointless tasks, and arbitrary punishment, and allows the school to feel more like a neighborhood institution and less an outpost of occupation.

39

ANIMATING THE BILL OF RIGHTS

William Estrada

Dana and I meet during her prep period to begin discussing what we would focus on during her 6th and 8th grade Social Studies class at Telpochcalli Elementary in the Little Village neighborhood in Chicago. Dana tells me that her focus will be on the Bill of Rights and goes on to explain that the lesson is getting stale and she wants to approach it in a new way. I was personally interested in experimenting with stop motion animation, as a way to use new media in the classroom. We discuss how we will introduce the theme, our timeline, student discussions, hands-on activities, and how the project will be shared with the school community. In preparation for class, Dana hands me a social studies book and I show her the animations I've done with other students.

We begin the new unit by reading the Pledge of Allegiance. Most students have a hard time reciting it and, when asked what it means, have a hard time explaining it. We break up the Pledge of Allegiance into sections and have students read each section aloud as a class; stopping periodically to interpret the section of the pledge we have just read. Students begin questioning whether we are a nation that is *indivisible* and *a nation with liberty and justice for all* that reside within it. Students feel that the pledge isn't a true representation of what they see in their communities or what they experience. We ask students to write a Pledge of Allegiance that encompasses the ideas in the original version with their own thoughts of what our nation should be. The following three examples represent the work that students created:

> I pledge to believe and never lose hope, on our nation on which we stand and to respect, love, believe, as much I can because that is the heart of a true American.

(Henry)

Animating the Bill of Rights 169

The Bill of Rights, Telpochcalli Elementary School, Chicago, 2011

I promise to help anyone no matter who they are, on things they can't do on their own. And also to help those who are from this nation but also help those who are not. To try and stop racism and hatred of the people who live in this land and on this world. To defend the weak and give strength to those who are strong. And to protect those who are victims and keep them safe.

(Jazmin)

I pledge allegiance to our flag of the United States. To all races and all beliefs of the entire Nation, to be indivisible with immigration, cultures, traditions, religions, languages, and freedom to the entire Nation.

(Kevin)

Using the Pledge of Allegiance as a starting point, students create postcards that visually represent what they have written. We gathered old and new magazines and began cutting, looking at composition, the relationship between text and image, and color to create a collage. At this point Lulua, my student teacher, joined us and began planning the next steps. First, we distributed handouts listing the ten Constitutional amendments. We discussed why the amendments were important when they were introduced and how they are important now. Second, students broke up into groups and chose only five rights that they believed were the most important. If the group couldn't agree on five, they would lose all their rights. Students began discussing which rights they thought were essential and why. Debates took place amongst the students and they began to discuss current events and personal experiences to support their arguments. After 40 minutes of heated debate, four of the five groups agreed on five rights. We discussed the challenges of choosing only five rights and how they came to an agreement. Students began to talk about freedom of speech and the right to peacefully assemble in immigration rallies, and the right to privacy and search and seizure from police and their parents. They used what they learned and applied it to their own experiences. Last, students were asked to partner up and choose one right to further explore.

We then discussed the stop motion animation process and how their animations would be used as public service announcements (PSAs). We showed sample PSAs via YouTube from Marwen students, blu, yannikronenberg, smartkid82504, QuarterPastWonderful, the Human Rights Action Center, and Amnesty International. Lulua had students create storyboards of their animations and asked them to think about what story they wanted to tell. Were the characters easy to relate to? Was the message clear and concise? When students finished their storyboards they met with me individually to create a stop motion animation sample using digital stills. Once they went through the process, they had a better understanding of what they needed to do. Students worked diligently on their stop motion animation and were constantly discussing how they should position the camera, how many frames they needed, and how the audience would perceive the message. Students would constantly review their stills and re-shoot if they didn't like it. Once finished, we met with each group individually to critique the work and make sure the animation and message was clear. Once everyone was satisfied with the work created, we uploaded the stills and began to edit them. I would meet with each individual group to edit their animations and create titles and credits.

Everyone was excited to see the animations come together. Students had a better understanding of their rights and were able to share their knowledge with others. During the 8th grade fundraiser, the DVD we created was shown to peers, teachers, parents, and school supporters. The animations were received with enthusiasm and many people were surprised that we could do animation with such social awareness within a school setting. Dana, Lulua, and I were proud of the work our students had accomplished; their ability to take the Bill of Rights and transform it into animations that related to their personal experiences was transformative for all of us. I was elated that students experimented with new media and in the process became more aware of the rights we hold as human beings in this country.

40

THINK TWICE, MAKE ONCE

Anne Thulson

When you walk into my school you might see a line of thigh-high, rubber gaiters for river-ecosystem fieldwork, a staff member's parent sharing her immigrant experience to a fifth grade class, or a small group of eight-year-olds comparing their research about Indian Boarding Schools from the Western History Museum.

We practice crossing borders at this K-8, expeditionary learning public school. Community members come into our building and we go outside of it to learn. Students uncover curriculum through long-term learning investigations. Thirty-three percent of our students receive free and reduced lunch and the mix of professional and working classes at our school is intentionally heterogeneous. This school culture is structured so students are not tracked, but work and think together through learning projects, using one another as valuable resources.

When our middle schoolers studied river ecosystems, they visited the Platte River weekly to assess the temperature, chemistry, and invertebrate population. They learned that taking a hot shower or doing a load of laundry could upset the delicate ecosystem of our city's river. This research became the context for a public art piece performed by my students.

Our integrated art curricula ask students to think and act poetically within their studies. So when students came into my art room with river science knowledge, we made a list of big ideas, like the untold story of the relationship between the natural world and human consumption. Then we investigated visual poets who work with this idea. Dominque Mazeaud in her *The Great Cleansing of the Rio Grande River* staged monthly performances to clean up the river. Radical puppet theaters like Bread and Puppet and Red Moon inform and enchant the public about the devastating effects of human consumption.

Middle-school students love masks and beg to make them. They are surrounded by bad examples like celebrities decorating masks for charity events or indigenous

Think Twice, Make Once 173

The Platte River Walk, The Odyssey School, 7th and 8th grades, Denver, Colorado, 2010

mask projects at summer camp that ignore or skim over socio-political contexts. Sometimes it is best to just say no to hackneyed projects like mask-making; however, these projects can present a useful opportunity for deconstructing and reconstructing historically faulty art-educational practices.

If we do make masks, we first spend a lot of time not making anything. We have discussions and conduct investigations about masks within various contexts and histories. We also spend a considerable amount of time looking at artists who have appropriated masks and contemporary ideas of ritual and performative actions using masks.

To start this Platte River project, we studied west African masks used in ceremonies to influence nature and humans. We focused on the mask wearer's transformation as a spiritual force to summon power over natural forces. We then examined the work of artists Pablo Picasso, Kehinde Wiley, and Fred Wilson.

Through Picasso we looked at how he appropriated indigenous masks for his own expressive, artistic journey and ignored the stories behind the original masks. We explored how his inspiration and admiration of the masks eclipsed any other story. Through Wiley's work, my students and I explored the phrase about his work that "interrogates the notion of the master painter." We used this phrase to interrogate the notion of the master Modernists like Picasso and their use of African and Oceanic masks. Then we looked at Wilson's work. By rearranging museum collections, he asks the viewer to look at stories other than the master narrative. We reflect on Wilson's piece *Picasso/Whose Rules?* in which he uses *Les Demoiselle D'Avignon* to ask questions about appropriation and the untold stories behind the dominant stories of art history.

Many questions arise out of our discussions to guide our researching and making: how will we tell our public about the hidden story of the Platte River? How will we appropriate the idea of transformative mask making in an informed way? What is implied when we appropriate? What does it mean to be informed about masks? How can we express through our masks the story of the interrelatedness of humans with nature?

Finally we are ready to make things. Students show their research of the river in their work, matching abstract ideas to symbol, metaphor and form. They work alone and in groups. The project required studio instruction on color theory, sewing, collage, assemblage, construction, repetition, balance, contrast, metaphor, and symbolism. Eventually our efforts will lead to creating masks or puppets that embody scientific ideas about water health to hopefully influence human behavior in their actions towards the river. And we'll wear them downtown on a river walk to raise public awareness of its ecosystem.

Their finished work included: symbolic spirals of interacting chemicals, critter-like micro and macro invertebrates, river spirit faces, good and evil fantasy figures, celestial beings and abstract forms representing water temperature, tableaus of the water cycle and landfills, and naturalistic wildlife.

Students drew diagram cards explaining their masks to inform the public we encountered on our walk. We also wrote a bill of health to read to the river based on the students' collective knowledge about its current ecosystem. At the time of their testing, the river was healthy with micro and macro invertebrates.

With six adult chaperones, we took our masks downtown and walked toward the river and through the city. En route, we handed our cards to wary and curious pedestrians. Cars honked, people waved or stopped to talk, and others ignored us.

Afterwards, students discussed their experience. Public interventions in our culture are usually about selling or proselytizing. We discussed how public art spectacle is free with no strings attached. One chaperone said she thought an Earth Day rally would be a more appropriate venue.

The chaperone's comment got me thinking. An Earth Day rally is exactly the venue I didn't want. That would not be an intervention. My students' procession interrupted and transformed the predictability of a public space. They disrupted business-as-usual. How is that different from interacting in an "appropriate" venue? Our interaction was unexpected. The results were unknown. We experienced the disequilibrium of our uncertain roles with our viewers, the joy when people were moved by our efforts, an affinity with nature, and meaningful, unexpected dialogue with strangers about the untold story of the river.

41
ART HISTORY AND SOCIAL JUSTICE IN THE MIDDLE-SCHOOL CLASSROOM

Kimberly Lane

Moments after the image went up on the screen all murmuring in my eighth grade classroom ceased. A beat of silence, then a clamoring of questions. "What is *that*?" "What's wrong with his hands?" "Why does he look like that?" "What does it mean?" Luba Lukova's image, *Censorship*, from her 2008 Social Justice portfolio was projected at the front of the darkened room. I knew I had their attention.

The School at Columbia University in New York City where I am the eighth grade art teacher is a K-8 school and has a concept-based curriculum. The curriculum addresses social justice in every subject, and teachers are committed to making meaningful interdisciplinary connections. Our administration supports our efforts through weekly curricular planning meetings. I am always aware of what is being taught in my students' English, science, social studies and other classes, which allows me to make authentic connections in my own classroom. Our eighth graders know that *The Quest for Social Justice* will be the overarching theme for their year. My weekly half-hour art history class focuses on artists whose work addresses this. Developmentally, social justice is an ideal theme for 13- and 14-year-olds. They are beginning to be more aware of justices and injustices in their own lives, their communities and the larger world. They carry their opinions fiercely and enjoy debating with each other and with their teachers.

The Social Action Project is the culminating project for the eighth graders. The students identify a topic of deep concern about which they can in some way "take action." They do thorough research and may choose any media to represent their learning for their final presentations. Each year several students choose visual art as a vehicle of expression, while others make videos, write and perform musically, and create displays or pamphlets to present the actions they have taken to make change in the world.

Luba Lukova, *Censorship*, 2008

In my art history class, I wanted to introduce visual artists who address issues of justice and injustice. Maria Martinez (2007) writes:

> Artists not only document social change; they promote, inform, and shape it. Art is the intellectual underpinning of social change; nowhere is there more potential and more need for art than here and now.
>
> (pp. 5–6)

I wondered if the students would agree? I selected artworks by contemporary artists such as Ester Hernandez, Alfredo Jaar, and Luba Lukova, as well as heavy hitters like Picasso's *Guernica* and Goya's *The Third of May 1808*. Each class was dedicated to one particular artist and usually focused on one specific piece. How would the students respond to these works of art? Would they feel that a work of visual art could be considered "social action" in and of itself?

With Lukova's print, we began with a dialogue-based inquiry into the piece. My go-to first question is, "Who can describe what we are seeing here?" Several students contributed comments: *A man is trying to play a flute. His face is contorted in pain. His fingers cannot move because they are nailed to the flute. The whole print is done in a palette of red, black and white. There is a black strip with the word "censorship" printed in the bottom right corner.*

Though I usually focus on one piece by each artist, I could not resist showing several images from Lukova's Social Justice 2008 portfolio of 12 posters including ones addressing privacy, the income gap, health care, war, and ecology. After discussions about the *Censorship* and *Privacy* prints, I put two questions to the students: what stands out to you most about Lukova's work? Do you think that her images are effective as efforts for social action? A rich discussion was cut short when class ended. Luckily, I had a platform for our conversation to continue.

Knowing that half an hour would not allow much time for discussion, I sought help from Karen Blumberg, an educational technologist at my school. Though I had no prior experience with web design, Karen quickly taught me how to use Google Sites to create a discussion forum for my eighth graders. Each lesson had its own page and I was able to upload images from my PowerPoint slides and post one or two questions to the students. For homework, each student was responsible for posting responses in the comments section.

It was clear from the responses that many of the students did consider Lukova's work to be "social action."

> I think that her images are effective for social action because they are so simple but are able to give powerful messages even without the words, and because of that they make you think about these pressing topics.
>
> *(Oscar)*

Unlike other artists, there aren't too many different ways to interpret her work, but it is still very powerful. It leaves you thinking about the issue ... rather than presenting a solution. The color and style of each image draws you to it in its simplicity. Lukova's work shows very complex issues in a very simple way.

(Michael)

Her images are effective, even if they don't change any specific practice. The fact that we are learning about her message at school shows that her work is teaching future generations, those who will be able to make a change.

(Zoe)

Often when we ask our students to do homework, they do it on their own, and the teacher reads and responds to it alone. With a website or blog, the experience is public; students must consider that responses are immediately available to classmates, the school community at large and, depending on access, possibly the world. With website discussion I am able to stretch the students' engagement with the material beyond our time in the classroom. I am convinced that students have greater investment in their responses because they are aware of the site's public nature. Luba Lukova herself came across our site independently, to our delight. Whether conversations like these take place in classrooms or online, they broaden our students' awareness of the power art has to promote change.

Reference

Martinez, M. X. (2007). The art of social justice. *Social Justice*, *34*(1), 5–11.

42

WHATEVER COMES NEXT WILL BE MADE AND NAMED BY US

Vanessa López-Sparaco

The first word that both my mother and I spoke in English was *acorn*. I was 6 years old; she was 38 years old. I grew up having to read and write for most of my elders who did not understand the language or the pace and structure of American culture, life, and its various systems. I made it through school, when so many others around me failed, because luck upheld my smarts. I had a few teachers who pitied me and even fewer that understood me. I needed an education that valued the strength within my struggle. I needed my experience to "coexist in a nonhierarchical way with the other ways of knowing" (hooks, 1994, p. 84). I needed my experience to be valued.

In *Teaching to Transgress*, bell hooks articulates the difference between education as a practice of freedom and education that merely strives to reinforce dominance (1994, p. 4). I teach because I fundamentally believe teaching is a form of active resistance and responsible revolution. I teach because I believe that education is political and thus power and dominance are inherent in its practice. It is imperative that we teach about and for social justice to create not only awareness, but balance.

Social justice is about creating for our students a sense of connection and responsibility to community and relevancy to the world around them. As an art educator, I believe the discipline must be tied to action in the world in a way that empowers students. Like me, many of my students have lived experiences that are not valued within the typical school setting. My classroom must then be the place that challenges hegemony and values multiple ways of knowing.

I currently teach at Roland Park Elementary Middle School (RPEMS). RPEMS is a large urban, public school located in Baltimore, Maryland. There are approximately 1200 students attending RPEM. Fifty percent of the students are African-American, 40 percent are Caucasian, 8 percent are Asian, almost 2 percent are Hispanic, and less than 1 percent are American Indian. In a segregated city, our school is truly diverse.

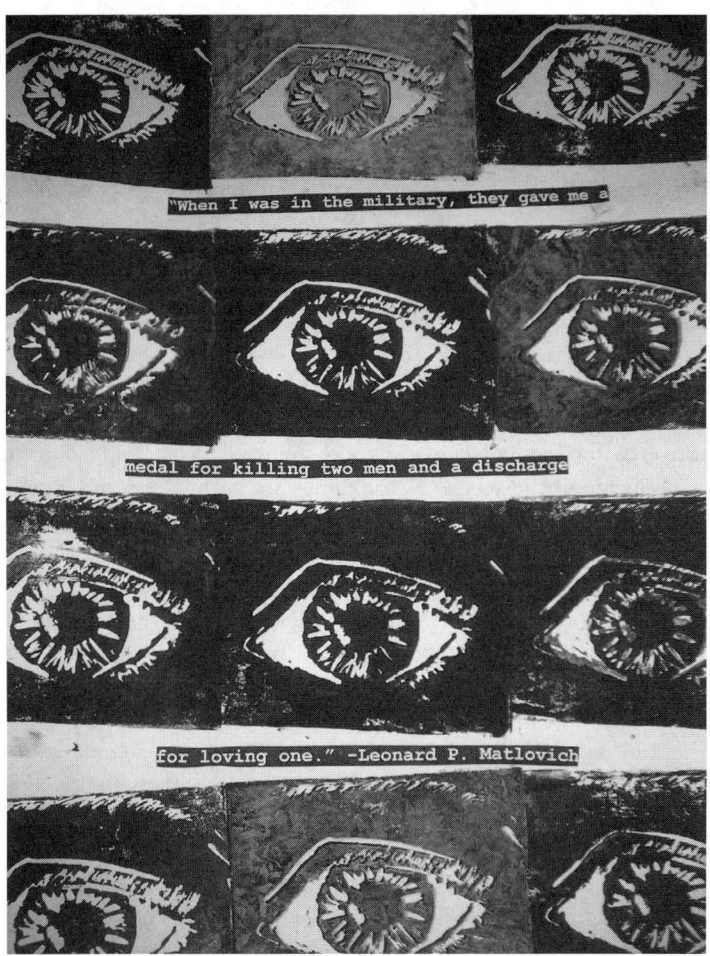

Maggie Ratrie, *Leonard P. Matlovich*, June 2010, print media, 12 × 18 in.

In my eighth grade elective class, we had previously done a unit on observational drawing and were now focusing on portraiture, more specifically self-portraits. Students began by doing various studies of different parts of their faces; eyes, nose, mouths. While students worked on their standard self-portraits, I was intrigued by the way they gazed at themselves in the mirror. I began to wonder, what have those eyes seen? From there I thought, how can I extend these observational and portrait projects into something more meaningful and relevant? I decided to have students focus solely on their eyes. I designed a unit incorporating observational drawing, printmaking and collage all centering on the theme of *The Eye*. I hoped that through this unit, I would better understand what social issues adolescents struggled with. Furthermore, I hoped through the unit to better understand and develop my role as facilitator of knowledge rather than dictator and to push my lessons towards action.

Students began by creating numerous eye studies; focusing on the individual shape and color of their eyes while simultaneously reflecting and journaling on various prompts. I asked students to reflect on the saying "eyes are the windows to the soul." We shared responses and then I had them go back and write about all the injustices they and their eyes have witnessed. I probed them to reflect on injustices witnessed and personally experienced. What things do you wish you could change in the world? What things are wrong with life as we live it? We went on to discuss the lack of public awareness and action around the various topics such as teen pregnancy, gang violence, domestic violence, and child abuse.

After intense conversations, we returned back to our eye drawings and now transferred them onto linoleum blocks. We discussed printmaking technique and positive and negative space. Students became so invested in their work and in each other's work that my role became minimal. Students printed their eye blocks to fill the entire paper. This alone was striking. Students then went on top of the black and layered the prints with additional colors of their choice. Following this, students blacked out an area—created a hole—a void—and used reappropriated images and/or text to discuss their chosen topic. Throughout the unit students were engaged and motivated. As a class we had extremely honest and intimate conversations. Opinions often differed, but the class created room for the tension. Students became genuinely interested in each other's topics and supportive of their peers. Again I took the backseat, only occasionally posing aesthetic questions or offering my opinion when asked. My students owned the classroom. Finally students contacted local organizations that advocated for their chosen topic; they interviewed personnel and in the end, decided to either donate their artwork to the organization or volunteer.

Colleagues were intrigued and disturbed. Some of the topics such as abortion and drug abuse had images that were hard for some to view. Ultimately some work was censored by the school administration because they deemed it not appropriate for the entire school. Even within all this, my students felt a profound sense of accomplishment with this unit. They were proud of their work and of our evolution as a class.

When students examine and create art about a social issue they feel passionately about, their voices are valued and they come to see themselves in others. Adolescents are still raw and able to see. Their eyes are open. Our job is to teach them to see the world as it is and as it could be. Whatever comes next will be made and named by us.

Reference

hooks, b. (1994). *Teaching to transgress: Education as the practice of freedom.* New York: Routledge.

CONTRIBUTORS

Volume Editors

Therese Quinn teaches and writes about the arts and public education. She is Chair and Associate Professor of Art Education at the School of the Art Institute of Chicago. Email: therese.quinn@gmail.com

John Ploof is an artist and Professor of Art Education at the School of the Art Institute of Chicago. Email: jploof@saic.edu

Lisa Hochtritt is a thrift store aficionado and Chair of Art Education at Rocky Mountain College of Art + Design (RMCAD) in Denver, Colorado. Email: Lisa.Hochtritt@gmail.com

Editors' Introduction—Image

Jim Duignan is an artist and professor of visual art and education at DePaul University. He founded the Stockyard Institute, a collaborative artist project and experimental teaching collective.

Foreword

Ryan Alexander-Tanner is a cartoonist and educator who lives in Portland, Oregon. www.ohyesverynice.com

Bill Ayers is an education/political activist who most recently co-authored *Teaching the Taboo*.

Maxine Greene, an educational philosopher, author, social activist, and teacher, founded the Maxine Greene Foundation for Social Imagination, the Arts, and

Contributors

Education in 2003. The foundation supports the creation and appreciation of works that embody fresh social visions.

Part I

Justseeds Artists' Cooperative is a decentralized network of 26 artists from the U.S., Canada, and Mexico who are committed to making print and design work that reflects a radical social, environmental, and political stance. Website: www.justseeds.org. *Cut and Paint* is a zine and website edited and maintained by Nicolas Lampert, Josh MacPhee, and Colin Matthes. *Cut and Paint*'s focus is the stencil, its ease of reproduction, and its role in the distribution of visual ideas. Website: www.cutandpaint.org

Josh MacPhee works with themes of history, radical politics, and public space. His most recent books are *Celebrate People's History! The Poster Book of Resistance and Revolution* (The Feminist Press, 2010) and *Signs of Change: Social Movement Cultures 1960s to Now* (co-edited with Dara Greenwald, AK Press, 2010). Website: www.justseeds.org

Colin Matthes is an interdisciplinary artist living in Milwaukee, Wisconsin. He also works collectively with Justseeds. Websites: http://colinmatthes.com/ and www.justseeds.org

David Darts is Chair of the Department of Art and Art Professions at New York University.

Heidi Cody is an artist and Professor at Pacific Northwest College of Art in Portland, Oregon. Website: http://heidicody.com

Kevin Tavin is an Associate Professor of Art Education at The Ohio State University. Email: tavin.1@osu.edu

Kutiman (Ophir Kutiel, born 1982) is a musician, composer, producer and animator from Israel. His online music video project ThruYOU, mixed from samples of YouTube videos, received more than 10 million views between 2009 and 2010.

K. Wayne Yang is an Assistant Professor in the Department of Ethnic Studies at the University of California San Diego (UCSD). Email: kwayne@ucsd.edu

ToroLab was founded in 1995 by Raúl Cárdenas Osuna in Tijuana BC, Mexico. It is a collective workshop/laboratory of contextual studies that identifies situations or phenomena of interest for research. Website: www.torolab.org

Contributors

Nato Thompson is a writer and curator who currently works as Chief Curator at the New York public art organization Creative Time.

Mequitta Ahuja makes large works on canvas and paper. Her work has been exhibited across the U.S. as well as in Paris, Brussels, Berlin, Dubai, and India. The artist's website is: www.automythography.com

Romi Crawford is Assistant Professor of Literature, Africana, and Visual Critical Studies in the Liberal Arts Department at the School of the Art Institute of Chicago. Email: rcrawf@saic.edu

Emily Jacir was born in Bethlehem, grew up in Saudi Arabia, went to high school in Italy, and received her university degrees in the United States. She currently lives and works in Ramallah and New York.

Edie Pistolesi is an art professor at California State University, Northridge. Email: edie.pistolesi@csun.edu

Paula Nicho Cúmez is a Maya Kaqchikel painter and a founding member of the Maya Kaqchikel Women's painting collective of San Juan de Comalapa, Guatemala.

Kryssi Staikidis is Associate Professor of Art and Design Education at Northern Illinois University in DeKalb, Illinois. Email: kstaikidis@niu.edu

Rafael Trelles is a Puerto Rican painter, drawer, performer, urban artist, and creator of installations. He lives and works in San Juan, Puerto Rico. Email: rafaeltrelles@gmail.com

Nicolas Lampert is a Milwaukee/Chicago based interdisciplinary artist and author. Collectively, he works with the Justseeds Artists' Cooperative (www.justseeds.org). His artist website is: www.machineanimalcollages.com

Doug Blandy is Associate Dean/Director of the Arts and Administration Program in the School of Architecture and Allied Arts at the University of Oregon.

Dipti Desai is Associate Professor and Director of the Art Education Program at New York University. Email: dd25@nyu.edu

Elizabeth Koch is a fourth grade teacher at Public School 3, New York, NY. Elizabeth can be reached at: BethMK@gmail.com

Robert W. Sweeny is Associate Professor of Art and Art Education at Indiana University of Pennsylvania. Email: sweeny@iup.edu

Hannah Johnston is an art teacher at Columbia Heights Educational Campus in Washington, DC. Email: hannah.liz12@gmail.com

Part II

Kaisa Leka is a Finnish comic artist and politician from Porvoo. Website www.kaisaleka.net

Carrie Sandahl is an Associate Professor at the University of Illinois at Chicago, specializing in disability art and culture. Email: csandahl@uic.edu

Darrel Morris is an artist and storyteller living in southeastern Kentucky. He has received the Louis Comfort Tiffany Fellowship and the Richard Driehaus Foundation Artist Award.

Dónal O'Donoghue is an Associate Professor and Chair of Art Education at the University of British Columbia, Vancouver, Canada. Email: donal.odonoghue@ubc.ca

Nicholas Galanin is a contemporary artist from Tlingit/Aleut, Sitka, Alaska. Website: http://galan.in

Anne-Marie Tupuola is an independent international academic, consultant and researcher who has recently relocated to New York from London, U.K. Email: amtupuola@yahoo.com

Kimsooja is an installation and video artist. In her work, everyday actions—sewing or doing laundry—become performative experiences. She was born in Taegu, Korea and now lives and works in New York. Website: www.kimsooja.com

Dalida María Benfield is a digital media artist, scholar, and activist, and is currently a Fellow at the Berkman Center for Internet and Society at Harvard University. Email: dmbenfield@cyber.law.harvard.edu

Xu Bing works out of his studios in Beijing and Brooklyn, and since 2008 has served as vice president of The Central Academy of Fine Arts (CAFA). Website: www.xubing.com

Buzz Spector is Dean of the College and Graduate School of Art in the Sam Fox School of Design and Visual Arts at Washington University in St. Louis. Email: spector@samfox.wustl.edu

Contributors 189

Bernard Williams is a painter, sculptor, muralist, and installation artist based in Chicago, Illinois. He is represented by the Thomas McCormick Gallery in Chicago.

James Haywood Rolling, Jr. is Chair and Dual Associate Professor of Art Education and Teaching and Leadership at Syracuse University. Website: http://syr.academia.edu/JamesHRollingJr

Hock E Aye Vi Edgar Heap of Birds teaches at University of Oklahoma since 1988 while lecturing/exhibiting his work in New York, Australia, India, China, Europe, Cheyenne/Arapaho and Dine Nations. Website: www.heapofbirds.com

Elizabeth Delacruz is Professor of Art Education at the University of Illinois at Urbana-Champaign. Email: edelacru@illinois.edu

Samuel Fosso is a Cameroonian photographer, born in 1962. He explores self-identity and portraiture through his work by taking on and documenting the roles of others. jean marc patras galerie: www.jeanmarcpatras.com

G. E. Washington is Visiting Assistant Professor of Art Education at The College of Saint Rose in Albany, New York. Email: garnellwashington@yahoo.com

Olivia Gude, Founding Director of Spiral Workshop, is a Professor at the University of Illinois at Chicago and a community-based public artist. Website: http://naea.digication.com/omg/

Miia Collanus is a lecturer in craft education in University of Helsinki. Email: miia.collanus@helsinki.fi

Tiina Heinonen studies in the textile teacher study program at the University of Helsinki in Finland. Email: tiina.i.heinonen@helsinki.fi

Korina Jocson is Assistant Professor of Education in the College of Arts and Sciences at Washington University in St. Louis. Email: kjocson@wustl.edu

Brett Cook is an artist, educator, and healer based in Berkeley, California. Website: www.brett-cook.com

Part III

Temporary Services is Brett Bloom, Salem Collo-Julin, and Marc Fischer. They are based in Chicago and Copenhagen and have existed, with several changes in membership and structure, since 1998. Temporary Services produces exhibitions, events, projects, and publications.

Harrell Fletcher is an Associate Professor of Art and Social Practice at Portland State University. He lectures and creates participatory projects around the world. Website: www.harrellfletcher.com

Juan Carlos Castro is Assistant Professor of Art Education at Concordia University in Montréal, Québec. Email: JuanCarlos.Castro@concordia.ca

Pinky & Bunny make *The Pinky Show* (www.PinkyShow.org), the original super lo-tech hand-drawn educational project. They are cats and live in the desert.

Steven Ciampaglia is an Assistant Professor of Art Education at Northern Illinois University. He can be reached at sciampaglia1@niu.edu

La Pocha Nostra is an interdisciplinary international arts organization based in San Francisco with branches, factions, and members in multiple cities and countries. Our common denominator is a desire to cross and erase dangerous borders between art and politics, practice and theory, artist, and spectator. Core members include: Guillermo Gómez-Peña, Roberto Sifuentes, Michele Ceballos, Dani d'Emilia, and Emma Tramposch. Website: www.pochanostra.com

Jorge Lucero is an artist and Assistant Professor of Art Education at The University of Illinois, Urbana-Champaign. Website: www.jorgelucero.com

Future Farmers/Amy Franceschini is a pollinator who creates formats for exchange and production that question and challenge the social, cultural and environmental systems that surround her. An overarching theme in her work is a perceived conflict between humans and nature. Website: www.futurefarmers.com

A. Laurie Palmer is an artist, writer, and Professor in Sculpture at the School of the Art Institute of Chicago. Website: www.resistantsubstances.net

Appalshop is a non-profit multi-disciplinary arts and education center in the heart of Appalachia. Its education and training programs support communities' efforts to solve their own problems in a just and equitable way. Website: http://appalshop.org/

Maritza Bautista is a bilingual (Tex-Mex, *pocha*) visual arts and video artist, educator and cultural worker.

Contributors

Navjot Altaf is an installation/video artist working with artists from different disciplines including indigenous artists from Bastar. She lives and works in Mumbai and Bastar.

Manisha Sharma is currently a doctoral candidate and teaching assistant in Art Education at The Ohio State University. Email: connect@manishasharma.com

Chiapas Photography Project (CPP) provides indigenous Maya people in Chiapas, Mexico with opportunities for cultural and artistic self-expression through photography. Website: http://chiapasphoto.org. Carlota Duarte is an artist who founded and directs the Chiapas Photography Project. Email: cduarte @rscj.org. Xunka' López Díaz is a Tzotzil indigenous photographer from Chiapas, Mexico, the author of *Mi Hermanita Cristina, una niña chamula.*

Lisa Yun Lee is the Director of the Jane Addams Hull-House Museum in Chicago and writes for *In These Times* Magazine. Email: lisalee@uic.edu

Dilomprizulike, popularly known as the Junkman from Afrika, is an international artist, performer, writer and teacher who makes sculptural installations as creative concepts and social commentaries from discarded items found on the street. Website: www.thejunkyardafrika.net

Raimundo Martins is Professor and Dean of the College of Visual Arts, Federal University of Goiás, in Goiânia, Brazil. Email: raimundomartins2005@yahoo.es

B. Stephen Carpenter, II is Professor of Art Education at The Pennsylvania State University. Email: bsc5@psu.edu

Marissa Muñoz is a Ph.D. student in the Centre for Cross Faculty Inquiry in Education at the University of British Columbia. Email: munozbertka415 @gmail.com

Carol Culp is an art and language teacher with the Toronto District School Board. Email: carculp@gmail.com

Rubén Gaztambide-Fernández is an Associate Professor and Co-Director of the Centre for Media and Culture in Education at the Ontario Institute for Studies in Education. Email: rgaztambide@oise.utoronto.ca

Sharif Bey is a Dual Assistant Professor in Art Education and Teaching and Leadership at Syracuse University. Email: shbey@syr.edu

Part IV

Graeme Sullivan is an artist, professor and Director, School of Visual Arts, The Pennsylvania State University. Website: www.streetworksart.com/

Maura Nugent is an English teacher. She co-founded the Social Justice Academy at Kelvyn Park High School in Chicago, Illinois.

Keith "K-Dub" Williams is an artist and art educator and lives in Oakland, California. He is founder and creator of Tha Hood Games youth art and skateboard festivals. Email: Kdubart@aol.com

Jesse Senechal is a doctoral student in educational research at Virginia Commonwealth University, Richmond, Virginia. Email: jessesenechal@gmail.com

Delaney Gersten Susie is an art teacher at Scott Joplin Elementary School in Chicago, Illinois. Email: ms.susie.art@gmail.com

Bert Stabler is a high-school art teacher, writer, curator, and artist in Chicago. His good intentions keep him warm at night.

William Estrada teaches at Telpochcalli Elementary School in programs funded by Chicago Arts Partnerships in Education and teaches in other CPS Schools through Art Resources in Teaching. Email: william@werdmvmntstudios.com

Anne Thulson is Assistant Professor of Art Education at Metropolitan State College of Denver and the former K-8 Art Studio Instructor at The Odyssey School in Denver, Colorado. Email: athulson@mscd.edu. Website: www.annethulson.com

Luba Lukova is an artist and designer based in New York. She is known internationally for her thought-provoking work dealing with issues of social justice. Website: www.lukova.net

Kimberly Lane is an art teacher at The School at Columbia University, an independent K-8 elementary school in New York City. Email: kimberly.lane @gmail.com

Vanessa López-Sparaco is an Art Educator at Roland Park Elementary Middle School (RPEMS), Baltimore, Maryland. Email: vlopez-sparaco@bcps.k12.md.us

FIGURE CREDITS AND PERMISSIONS

Foreword	Comics by Ryan Alexander-Tanner
0.1	*Pedagogical Factory: Exploring Strategies for an Educated City* (2007). Courtesy of Jim Duignan.
I.1	*Ellen Gates Starr* (1900). Courtesy of the Library of Congress, Prints & Photographs Division LC-B2- 4088–11 [P&P]
1.1a	*Bike*, stencil (2004–2007) by Janet Attard. Courtesy of cutandpaint.org
1.1b	*Rat Race*, stencil (2004–2007) by Sue Simensky Bietila. Courtesy of cutandpaint.org
1.1c	*Rights-f*, stencil (2004–2007) by Sarah Healey. Courtesy of cutandpaint.org
1.1d	*The City is Yours*, stencil (2004–2007) by Icky A. Courtesy of cutandpaint.org
1.1e	*Garden*, stencil (2004–2007) by Andalusia. Courtesy of cutandpaint.org
1.1f	*Ant*, stencil (2004–2007) by Roger Peet. Courtesy of cutandpaint.org
3.1	Screen-shot from *The Mother of All Funk Chords, ThruYOU*, digital video mash-up (2009) by Kutiman. Courtesy of the artist
4.1	*COMA*, ink on pencil (2006) by Raúl Cárdenas Osuna at ToroLab. Courtesy of the artist
6.1	Detail of *Munir* from the *Where We Come From* series by Emily Jacir (2001–2003). Courtesy of Alexander and Bonin, New York. Photo by Bill Orcutt
6.2	Detail of *Munir* from the *Where We Come From* series by Emily Jacir (2001–2003). Courtesy of Alexander and Bonin, New York. Photo by Bill Orcutt

194 Figure Credits and Permissions

7.1	*Cánto a la Naturaleza* (Song to Nature) (2005) by Paula Nicho Cúmez. Courtesy of Joseph Johnston, Arte Maya Tz'utuhil
8.1	*Helicopter and Butterflies*, water-washed concrete (2005) by Rafael Trelles. Courtesy of the artist. Photo by Johnny Betancourt
9.1	*Northgate Peace and Forgiveness Garden* in Salem, Oregon (2010). Photo by Lauren Silberman
10.1	*Watch and Learn (Or Not!)*, iMovie shown on MacBook (May 2010) by Elizabeth Koch. Courtesy of the artist. Photo by Elizabeth Koch
11.1	*The War is Over*, signs on California highways (2004–2008) by Freewayblogger. Courtesy of Freewayblogger
II.1	Vogue Evolution photograph. Courtesy of the artists
12.1	*I Get Excited* from *I Am Not These Feet* (2003) by Kaisa Leka. Courtesy of the artist
13.1	*Men Don't Sew in Public: Made in the USA, Cushion #3* (2000) by Darrel Morris. Courtesy of Darrel Morris
14.1	Detail from the *Imaginary Indian* series, in wood, paint, and wallpaper (2009) by Nicholas Galanin. Courtesy of the artist
15.1	*Cities on the Move—2727 km Bottari Truck*, giclée print on Hahnemüele paper (2007) by Kimsooja. Courtesy of Kimsooja Studio
16.1	*Introduction to Square Word Calligraphy* and *Square Word Calligraphy Red Line Tracing Book* (1996) by Xu Bing. Courtesy of Xu Bing Studio
17.1	*Buffalo Chart*, painted wood and found objects (2009) by Bernard Williams. Courtesy of Bernard Williams
18.1	Detail of *Beyond the Chief*, 12-panel public art installation of signage (defaced). Courtesy of Hock E Aye Vi Edgar Heap of Birds
20.1	*It's the End of the World As We Know It*, cut black paper and ink jet prints on wall (2008) by teen artists and teachers of the (Dis)Order group in Spiral Workshop. Courtesy of Olivia Gude
21.1	*Textile Crafts for Girls, Woodwork for Boys?* picture collage (2010) by Tiina Heinonen and Saara Kumpulainen. Courtesy of Tiina Heinonen and Saara Kumpulainen. Photo by Tiina Heinonen
22.1	*Coloring Pauli Murray at The Pauli Murray Birthday Celebration*, paint pen and oil pastel on non-woven media (November 2007) by Brett Cook. Courtesy of the artist. Photo by Brett Cook
22.2	*Recognizing Different Worlds: Art, Social Change, and Documentary*, (Spring 2008) by Brett Cook. Courtesy of the artist. Photo by Brett Cook
III.1	*Designated Drivers*, digital media (2011) by Temporary Services. Courtesy of Temporary Services
23.1	*The Problem of Possible Redemption* (2003) by Harrell Fletcher. Courtesy of Harrell Fletcher

Figure Credits and Permissions 195

24.1	*Pinky Visits the Principal's Office*, *Pinky Show* comic number 5 (2011) by Pinky & Bunny. © Associated Animals Inc., a 501(c)3 non-profit educational organization. Courtesy of the artists
25.1	La Pocha Nostra. Courtesy of La Pocha Nostra. Photo by Zach Gross
26.1	*Rainwater Harvester/Greywater System Feedback Loop*, wood, steel, plastic, mint, and rubber (2007) by Amy Franceschini and Michael Swaine. Courtesy of the artists. Photo by Futurefarmers
27.1	Shot of Rick DiClemente filming Dewey Thompson for the documentary *Chairmaker*, 16mm color film (1975). Courtesy of Appalshop, Inc. Photo by Mimi Pickering
28.1	Detail from *Delhi Loves Me?*, (2005) by Navjot Altaf. Courtesy of the artist
29.1	*Untitled* (2000) by Emiliano Guzmán Meza. Courtesy of Carlota Duarte, Chiapas Photography Project. Photo by Emiliano Guzmán Meza
31.1	*Water Filter Production Demonstration as Public Pedagogy* (2007) by Texas A & M University. Courtesy of the TAMU Water Project
33.1	Excerpt from *Fat Albert is Not a Compliment*, pen and found image (2010) by Emily Puccia Colasacco. Courtesy of the artist
33.2	*Poser*, digital media (2010) by Justin Magnotta. Courtesy of the artist
IV.1	*Streetwalks: Inside LA III*, discarded timber frame, sheetrock, canvas, and wire (2010) by Graeme Sullivan. Courtesy of the artist. Photograph by Mary Sullivan
35.1	*Hood Games #1*, graphic design by Ryan Espinosa, art direction by K-Dub (2005). Courtesy of Keith "K-Dub" Williams, Barbara Murden, and Hood Games LLC.
36.1	*ROAR #1*, silkscreen (1997) by Jason Alforo. Courtesy of the artist
37.1	*Miracle on 79th Street* (2011) by students of Scott Joplin School, Chicago, IL. Courtesy of Delaney Gersten Susie
38.1	*Solar Powered Inflatable Exotic and Endangered Species Project* (2010) by students at B.E.S.T. High School. Courtesy of Bert Stabler
39.1	Screen-shot from *The Bill of Rights* (2011) by Telpochcalli Elementary School, Chicago, IL. Courtesy of William Estrada
40.1	*The Platte River Walk* (2010) by the Odyssey School, 7th and 8th grade, Denver, CO. Courtesy of Anne Thulson. Photo by Anne Thulson
41.1	*Censorship* (2008) by Luba Lukova. Courtesy of Luba Lukova
42.1	*Leonard P. Matlovich*, print media (2010) by Maggie Ratrie. Courtesy of Vanessa López-Sparaco. Photo by Vanessa López-Sparaco with permission from the artist Maggie Ratrie

Color Plates

1. *Learn About Black Panther Party History*, silkscreen (2010) by Nicolas Lampert. Courtesy of the artist
2. *American Alphabet*, aluminum light boxes with Lambda Duratrans prints (2000) by Heidi Cody. Courtesy of the artist
3. Screen-shot from *The Mother of All Funk Chords, ThruYOU*, digital video mash-up (2009) by Kutiman. Courtesy of the artist
4. *Emergency Architecture* project, "*S.O.S. Emergency Architecture*," digital image (2001) by Raúl Cárdenas Osuna at ToroLab. Courtesy of the artist
5. *Afrogalaxy*, enamel on paper (2007) by Mequitta Ahuja with assistance from Blue Sky Project. Courtesy of the artist and Blue Sky Project
6. *Memorial to 418 Palestinian Villages which were Destroyed, Depopulated and Occupied by Israel in 1948*, refugee tent and embroidery thread (2001) by Emily Jacir. Collection: National Museum of Contemporary Art-EMST, Athens. Courtesy of the artist. Photo by Emily Jacir
7. *Cruzando Fronteras* (Crossing Borders) (2007) by Paula Nicho Cúmez. Courtesy of Joseph Johnston, Arte Maya Tz'utuhil
8. Rafael Trelles working on *War Plane and Dove*, water-washed concrete (2005). Courtesy of the artist. Photo by Andrés Nieves
9. Cover from *I Am Not These Feet* (2003) by Kaisa Leka. Courtesy of the artist
10. *You Promised Me*, found fabric, sewing thread, and canvas (1993) by Darrel Morris. Courtesy of Darrel Morris
11. *Imaginary Indian*, in wood, paint, and wallpaper (2009) by Nicholas Galanin. Courtesy of the artist
12. *Mumbai: A Laundry Field*, C-Print (2007) by Kimsooja. Courtesy of Kimsooja Studio
13. *Book from the Sky*, hand printed books, ceiling and wall scrolls printed from wood letterpress (1987–1991) by Xu Bing. Courtesy of Xu Bing Studio
14. *Charting America*, painted wood and found objects (2010) by Bernard Williams. Photo by Doug Carr
15. Detail of *Beyond the Chief*, 12-panel public art installation of signage (defaced). Courtesy of Hock E Aye Vi Edgar Heap of Birds
16. *La femme libérée américaine dans des années 70* (1997) by Samuel Fosso. © Samuel Fosso. Courtesy jean-marc patras/galerie, Paris
17. *The Problem of Possible Redemption* (2003) by Harrell Fletcher. Courtesy of Harrell Fletcher
18. Screen-shot from *Ant Appeal: "Please Respect All Animals,"* an episode of *The Pinky Show* (2006). © Associated Animals Inc., a 501(c)3 non-profit educational organization. Courtesy of the artists
19. La Pocha Nostra. Courtesy of La Pocha Nostra. Photo by Zach Gross

20a *Victory Gardens Located Across From City Hall* (1943). Courtesy of the San Francisco History Center, San Francisco Public Library
20b *Victory Gardens* (2007) by Amy Franceschini/Future Farmers. Courtesy of the artist. Photo by Amy Franceschini
21 From *Stranger with a Camera*, 16mm color film finished on video (2000) by Appalshop. © Appalshop, Inc. Courtesy of Appalshop, Inc.
22 From *Delhi Loves Me?* (2005) by Navjot Altaf. Courtesy of the artist
23 *Untitled* (2000) by Xunka' López Díaz. Courtesy of Carlota Duarte, Chiapas Photography Project. Photo by Xunka' López Díaz
24 *Face of the City 1*, mixed media/installation (2006) by Dilomprizulike. Courtesy of the artist

Lyrics

Editors' Introduction	Gwendolyn Brooks, lyrics reprinted by consent of Brooks Permissions
	FM Supreme, lyrics from *This is A Movement*, on *The Beautiful Grind* LP (2008), forevermaroonpublishing, ASCAP
Part III Introduction	Billy Bragg, lyrics from *I don't need this pressure Ron* on the *Days Like These* LP (1985), GO DISCS. Courtesy of Billy Bragg

INDEX

activist artists 19, 104, 148
Addams, Jane xxii, 3
advertising 9–10, 25–27; environmental 27
aesthetic or political research 16
Africa 122–123
Afrogalaxy 17–18
Ahuja, Mequitta 5, 17–18, 187
Alexander-Tanner, Ryan xi–xvi, 185
Altaf, Navjot 99, 116–118, 191
alternative scrapbooking 80
American Alphabet 9–10
Anderson, Walter Truett 70
animation *see* cartoons; stop motion animation
Appalshop 99, 113–115, 190
art and politics 37, 122–123
artists' collectives 6, 14, 99, 107, 110
art teacher's role 79, 83,149, 158, 182
"art worlds" 30
authority, redistribution of 149, 155
Ayers, Bill xxi, xi–xvi, 185

Banksy 25
Barret, Elizabeth 113
Bautista, Maritza 99, 113–115, 190
Becker, H.S. 30
Benfield, Dalida María 51, 62–64, 188
Beyond the Chief 71–73
Bey, Sharif 99, 136–141, 191
Bill of Rights 168–171
biomythography 17
biopower 41, 44, 46
Blackness for Sale 43

Blandy, D. & Congdon, K.G. 32
Blandy, Doug 5, 28–34, 187
blogs 179
Blue Sky Project 17–18
body as medium 44, 53–55, 62, 64
Bolin, P.E. & Blandy, D. 28
Book from the Sky 65
Bragg, Billy 97
bumper stickers 116–118
Butler, J. 56

Cahan, S. and Kocur, Z. xxi
calligraphy 65–67
Carpenter, B.S. 99, 124–130, 137, 191
cartoons 53–55, 104
Castro, Juan Carlos 99, 101–103, 190
Celebrate People's History! 6
Censorship 176–179
Chin, Mel 126, 128
Chiapas Photography Project 99, 119–121, 191
Ciampaglia, Steven 99, 104–106, 190
classroom, outside of 9, 78, 137, 166–167, 172, 179
cleaning as art 25
clothing 14, 16, 24, 53, 155
Cody, Heidi 5, 9–10, 186
Collaboration 89–94, 124–130
collaborative ethnography 30–32
Collanus, Miia 52, 83–88, 189
commercial images 9
commons: Creative Commons 41, 44; definition of xxi; owned by the corporation 13; space of 41

community, bringing into the school 162
community events 155
conscientization 126
consumerism 10
context, art engaging with xx, xxi
Cook, Brett 52, 89–94, 189
cooptation of images by the media 38
corporate visual culture 9–10; logos 27
Cortez, J. xxi
Crawford, Romi 5, 17–18, 187
Creative Commons 41, 44
critical art education xxi
"critical gaze" 86–87
"cropped identity" 45
Crossing Borders 22
Culp, Carol 99, 131–135, 191
cultural recognition 147, 160–163
Cut & Paint series 6–7

Darts, David 5, 6–8, 186
Delacruz, Elizabeth 51, 71–73, 189
Delpit, Lisa 162
democracy 13, 35, 38
Desai, Dipti 5, 35–38, 187
Dewey, J. xxi
Dewhurst, M. xxi
digital consumerism 43
Dilomprizulike 122–123, 191
direct activism 107
disability arts 53
disability rights xxi
Discipline-Based Art Education (DBAE) xx, xxi
discussion forum 178–179
disembodiment 43
Disu, J. xxii
diverse student populations 136–141, 160
documentaries 150–152
documentary photography 121
Douglass, F. xxi
Duignan, Jim xix, 185

"economies of cognitive capitalism" 37
education, corporatization of 37
environmental justice 99, 124–130
Estrada, William 145, 168–171, 192
exhibition design 32–33
"expeditionary learning" 148
eyes 182–183

Facebook 45, 99
Face Up 94
Fairey, Shepard 25
feminism xxi, 83

Femme Americaine Liberee, La 74–75
filmmaking 113, 150
Finland 83–88
Fletcher, Harrell 99, 101–103, 190
flying 22
FM Supreme xxii
Fosso, Samuel 51, 74–75, 189
Foucault, M. 41, 44
Franceschini, Amy 110, 111, 190
Fraser, Nancy xx
free speech 44
Freewayblogger 38
Freire, P. 32, 79, 126
Future Farmers 110–112, 190

Galanin, Nicholas 51, 59, 188
Gaudelius, Y. and Speirs, P. xxi
Gaztambide-Fernández, Rubén 99, 131–135, 191
gender 56–58, 83–88
Gleick, Peter 127
global capitalism 10
green capitalism 27
Greene, Maxine xi–xvi, xxi, 99, 148, 185–186
Gude, Olivia 51, 76–82, 189
gum desk, the 39

Hardt, M. & Negri, A. 44
Heap of Birds, Edgar (Hock E Aye Vi) 51, 71–73, 189
Heinonen, Tiina 52, 83–88, 189
Hernandez, Manny 126
hieroglyphics 68–70
hip-hop 49, 61, 153
Hochtritt, Lisa xviii–xxii, 97–100, 185
homelessness 19–21, 166
Homework 35, 37, 38
hooks, bell 180
Hull-House 3
human rights 124, 126, 168–171
Hyde, L. xxi

I Am Not These Feet 53, 54
identity: biomythography 17; "cropped" 45; cultural 51, 70, 145; formation 135; gender 11, 55, 56, 58; personal 43, 59, 70, 137, 140; politics 50
identity script 59
Imaginary Indian 59–61
immigrant rights xviii, 22–24
India 116–118
indigenous people 22–24, 59, 71, 119
inklings 79–80

"institutions of isolation" 162
Internet 43, 87, 99, 148 *see also* Facebook; websites; YouTube
intersection of art and politics 19
interventionist strategy 51
i-Ronic 80
Israel 19–21

Jacir, Emily 5, 19–21, 187
Jackson, S. 44, 45
Jay-Z 49, 52
Jeremijenko, Natalie 126, 128
Jocson, Korina 52, 89–94, 189
Johnston, Hannah 5, 41–46, 188
"Junkman from Afrika" 122–123, 191
Justseeds Artists' Cooperative 5, 6–8, 186

Kiernan, B. 24
Kimsooja 51, 62–64, 188
"knowledge as struggle" 38
Koch, Elizabeth 5, 38–40, 187
Kutiman 5, 11–13, 186

Lampert, Nicolas 5, 25–27, 187
Lane, Kimberly 148, 176–179, 192
Lassiter, L.E. 30–31, 34
Lee, Lisa Yun 99, 119–121, 191
Leka, Kaisa 50, 53–55, 188
lived-experiences 137, 180
Livingston, Jennie 74
López-Sparaco, Vanessa 147, 180–183, 192
Lorde, Audre 17–18
Lucero, Jorge 99, 107–109, 190
Lukova, Luba 148, 176–179, 192

MacPhee, Josh 6–8, 186
Marshall, J. 45
Martins, Raimundo 99, 122–123, 191
mask-making 174–175
material culture 28, 30, 34
Matthes, Colin 186
Mazeaud, Dominque 172–175
Men Don't Sew in Public 56–58
Morris, Darrel 51, 56–58, 188
motivation 166
multicultural theories xxi
Muñoz, Marissa 99, 124–131, 191
music 11–13, 49, 61

Nakamura, L. 43
new creative forms 18
New Museum xxi
Nicho Cúmez, Paula 5, 22–24, 187

Nieto, S. xviii, 140
Northgate Peace and Forgiveness Garden 28–34
Nugent, Maura 145, 150–152, 192

Obadike, K. & M. 43
Ode to Lost Enthusiasm 39
O'Donoghue, Dónal 50, 56–58, 188
ownership 44

Palestinians 19–21
Palmer, A. Laurie 99, 110–112, 190
"parallel activities" 107
Patchwork Girl 44
Pedagogical Factory xix, xxii
performance art 107–109
photographs 74–75, 80, 119, 121
Picasso, Pablo 174, 178
Pinky Show, The 99, 104–106, 190
Pistolesi, Edie 5, 19–21, 187
Pledge of Allegiance 168
Ploof, John xviii–xxii, 49–52, 185
Pocha Nostra, La 99, 107–109, 190
politics of representation 59
Principles of Possibility 80
printmaking 182
Problem of Possible Redemption 101–103
public art 99, 116–118, 164–167; spectacle 175

queerness 51, 74–75
Quinn, Therese xviii–xxii, 3–5, 185

Rainwater Harvester/Greywater System Feedback Loop 110–111
realness 74–75
Reed, T.V. 30
refugees 19–21
relational art xxii
relational inquiry 51
rethinking, ways of 35
reversing type 51
rickshaws 116–118
Riis, Jacob 121
river ecosystems 172–175
ROAR 156–159
Rogoff, I. xxii, 37, 38
Rolling Jr., James Haywood 51, 68–70, 189
Roy, Arundhati 119

sampling 49
Sandahl, Carrie 50, 53–55, 188
Schubert, W.H. 97

sculpture 16, 51, 56, 59–61, 71, 110, 122, 166
self-portraits 51, 74–75, 131, 182
Senechal, Jesse 149, 156–159, 192
Sepúlveda, Beto xviii
settlement houses 3
sewing 19, 56–58, 85, 188
Sharma, Manisha 99, 116–118, 191
signs 41, 68, 71–73, 116, 161
skateboarding 153–155
Skin 43–44, 45
Skype 37
social imagination xiii, 185
social justice: artists who demonstrate 6, 8, 24, 25, 75, 126, 140; goals of xx; movements xxi, 27, 28, 30, 34; teaching for xx–xxii, 3, 46, 147, 150, 163, 176, 180
social media 41–46, 99 *see also* Facebook; YouTube
social movements, engaging with 30, 34
social reconstructionist theories xxi
socio-cultural contexts 33, 52, 83, 134
Sontag, Susan 121
spaces of inquiry 78
Spector, Buzz 51, 65–67, 188
Spiral Workshop 51, 76–82, 189
Spivak, G. 35, 37, 38
Square Word Calligraphy 66–67
Stabler, Bert 147, 164–167, 192
Staikidis, Kryssi 5, 22–24, 187
Starr, Ellen Gates 3
state censorship 13, 45
Steiner, D. 35, 37
stencils 6–8, 25–26
stereotypes 11, 59, 70, 113, 139
stop motion animation 168–170
street art 25–27, 153, 155
student voice 150–152, 155
Sullivan, Graeme 145–149, 192
Susie, Delaney Gersten 145, 160–163, 192
Sweeny, Robert W. 5, 41–46, 187

tattoos 43–44
Tavin, Kevin 5, 9–10, 186

teacher experiences 145
teaching and politics 180
Temporary Services 98, 99, 189–190
testing 38–39
textiles 51, 83–88
"Tha Hood Games" 153–155, 192
theory-practice dichotomy 52, 87, 131–135
Thompson, Nato 5, 14–16, 187
Thulson, Anne 148, 172–175, 192
ToroLab 5, 14–16, 186
transformation 91
Trelles, Rafael 5, 25–27, 187
Tupuola, Anne-Marie 51, 59–61, 188

unlearning 35, 37

Victory Gardens 110, 112
videos 11–13, 62, 101–103, 113, 150
Vieques 25–27
vogue dancing 51, 74–75
Vogue Evolution dance crew 50

wallpaper 59–60
War is Over, The 41–42, 43
Washington, G.E. 51, 74–75, 189
water 124–130
websites 179 *see also* Internet
Wei, D. 140
weirdness 76–82
Welsh, P.H. 31–32
Whitman, Walt 5
Williams, Bernard 51, 68–70, 189
Williams, Keith "K-Dub" 147, 153–155, 192
Wilson, Fred 139, 140, 174
Wukich, Richard 127

xenophobia 137
Xu Bing 51, 65–67, 188

Yang, K. Wayne 5, 11–13, 186
Young, Iris Marion xx
YouTube 11–13, 99, 104, 170

zines 156–159